SECRET COPENHAGEN

Johanne Steenstrup and Klaus Dahl

JonGlez

We have taken great pleasure in drawing up
Secret Copenhagen and hope that through its guidance
you will, like us, continue to discover unusual, hidden
or little-known aspects of the city.
Descriptions of certain places are accompanied
by thematic sections highlighting historical details
or anecdotes as an aid to understanding the city in all
its complexity.
Secret Copenhagen also draws attention to the multitude
of details found in places that we may pass every day
without noticing. These are an invitation to look more
closely at the urban landscape and, more generally,
a means of seeing our own city with the curiosity
and attention that we often display while travelling
elsewhere …

Comments on this guidebook and its contents, as well as
information on places we may not have mentioned, are
more than welcome and will enrich future editions.
Don't hesitate to contact us:
• Éditions Jonglez, 17, boulevard du Roi,
  78000 Versailles, France
• E-mail: info@jonglezpublishing.com

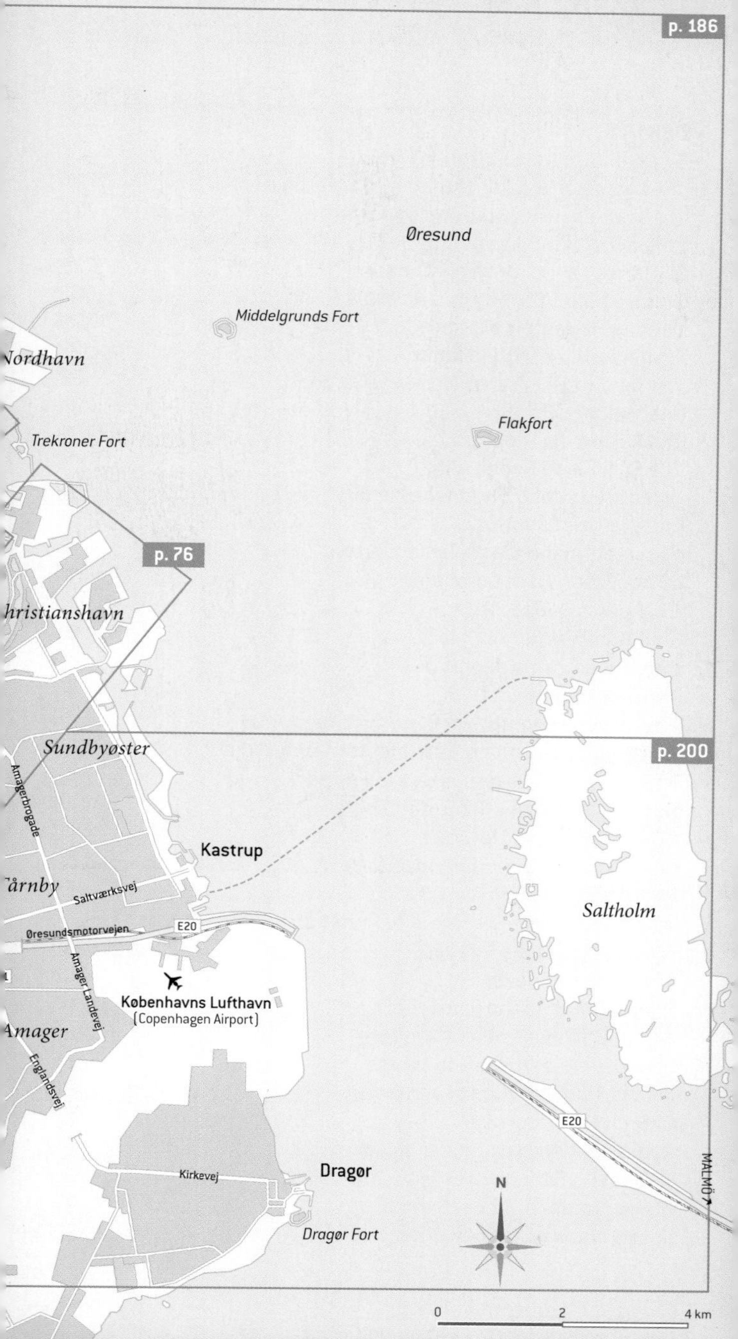

p. 186

Øresund

Middelgrunds Fort

Nordhavn

Flakfort

Trekroner Fort

p. 76

hristianshavn

Sundbyøster

p. 200

Amagerbrogade

Kastrup

årnby Saltværksvej

Saltholm

Øresundsmotorvejen E20

Amager Landevej

✈

Englandsvej

Københavns Lufthavn
(Copenhagen Airport)

Amager

E20

MALMÖ

Kirkevej

Dragør

N

Dragør Fort

0   2   4 km

CONTENTS

CONTENTS

OUTSIDE THE CENTRE SOUTH

CENTRE

SWASTIKAS IN THE GLYPTOTEK GARDEN ❶

Behind Ny Carlsberg Glyptotek, Dantes Plads 7, 1556 V
• Access from Tietgensgade, Ved Glyptoteket or Niels Brocks Gade
• S-train: Copenhagen Central Station

The remodelling of Carlsberg's former trademark

If you make your way to the Glyptotek Garden you will get to the 1906 extension, designed by the architect Hack Kampmann. Look up and you will see two swastikas carved beside each of the two windows at either end of the building.

In 1881, Carl Jacobsen, the owner of the Carlsberg Brewery, chose the swastika as the company trademark. There was nothing strange about this as, at the time when they were carved, the swastika had no Nazi connotations.

In fact, the swastika "wheel" has been used as a symbol of life and rebirth by many cultures since ancient times, among them those of the Hindus and Buddhists. Its association with Nazism came later, which explains why some of the other swastikas on the building were redesigned at some point in the 1930s: the symbols around the windows facing the crowded streets at the side were extensively remodelled to the point that they appear to be abstract carvings devoid of any symbolic meaning. But why were the ones facing the garden not reworked as well? It's a mystery.

THE SWASTIKA: A SYMBOL THAT PREDATES THE NAZIS

The swastika, a sacred symbol for thousands of years, is found in many ancient civilisations: among the Celts and Etruscans, in Northern Europe, Central America (Maya) and North America (Navajo Indians), and in Asia (mainly China, Tibet and India). Some believe that Tibet was the true (natural) origin of the symbol: the cross would simply be "drawn" on the slopes of the mythical Mount Kailash in western Tibet, sacred to Hindus and Buddhists and thought to be the source of the world's energy.

It is important to distinguish between *swástika* and *sowástika* (in Pali and Tibetan) – in Western languages, *swastika* and *sauvastika*. The sauvastika cross rotates to the left and is considered sinister and regressive by Eastern religions and the peoples of Western antiquity who, on the contrary, used the swastika rotating to the right as a benevolent and evolutionary symbol. Adolf Hitler and his peers appropriated this symbol and made it an evil sauvastika.

Thus the direction of rotation of the swastika or sauvastika determines its direct astronomical and cosmic significance: in a clockwise direction, positive, solar, it symbolises Universal Evolution and is typified by the swastika adopted by Charlemagne. In an anti-clockwise direction, negative, lunar, it indicates Planetary Involution and, in a more immediate context, the intention of subjecting the timeless and sacred to the strictly temporal and profane space, as typified by the sauvastika adopted by Hitler.

Because of the arms of the cross (*crux gammata*, after the Greek letter *gamma*), branches that leave behind a fiery trail as they turn, the swastika is the symbol of Universal Action. In this sense, it has always accompanied the graphic, pictorial or carved image of the saviours of humanity, the messiahs or avatars such as Christ. Christ is depicted in the ancient Roman catacombs at the centre of a spiral-shaped swastika because he represents the Spiritual Centre or Pole where the Supreme God resides who gave rise to the gods, mankind and other living beings. In short, it is the symbol of the Creator around which are arranged hierarchies of beings emanating from his unique Centre (Bindu, Sanskrit for "point" or "dot").

Like Christ, the Anointed One, who is the Mystical Centre of Christianity, Buddha, the Enlightened One, marks the Mystical Pole of the Buddhist faith, indicated in mankind through the Heart, the expression of spiritual consciousness, a sufficient reason for many Buddha images to have a swastika engraved on their chest. The Saivite Hindus, for their part, depict the god Shiva accompanied by a swastika. And although this symbol often appears on religious images in the East and even in the West with the reverse movement of the sauvastika, this can be attributed to the artist's ignorance. Like a reflection in the mirror it contradicts reality, because the swastika is the Spiritual Pole of mankind, the world and the universe, while the sauvastika expresses the opposite, the Material Pole of mankind, the world and the universe.

THE STAINED GLASS WINDOWS
IN THE FORMER *OVERFORMYNDERIET*

The Child and Youth Administration building (formerly the *Overformynderiet*)
Stormgade 18, 1555 V
• Contact the reception desk on the ground floor
• S-train: Copenhagen Central Station

The fragility of motherhood

I n the lobby of the former *Overformynderiet* (The Public Trustee's Office), the beautiful stained glass windows on the staircase depict a group of women with their children in a medieval church. The colours are luminous and beautiful and the power of maternal love is shown with great intensity.

There are some older children at the front of the procession but most of the figures are of mothers holding their babies. Some are asleep, others are just cuddling into their mothers, so their faces can't be seen. Except, that is, for one little girl in the middle panel. Both she and her mother look directly at any observers and are presented in a completely different way to the others. It is as if this particular mother is trying to tell us something.

The stained glass is the work of Agnes Slott-Møller (1862–1937) and was based on a sketch approved by Hans Holm, the architect who designed the building in 1901. The chosen subject of mothers and their children can be interpreted as symbolic of the care and protection provided by the *Overformynderiet*, a public institution which managed the funds and acted as trustees for minors and missing persons. But the subject matter also tells a personal story: the woman in the middle, who looks sternly out, is in fact the artist herself. In front of her stands her 7-year-old daughter Lykke and, in her arms, she holds her youngest daughter, Benedetta.

For Agnes Slott-Møller it was a challenge to be both a female artist and a mother at a time when the bourgeoisie saw motherhood as the most prestigious, and, in fact, the only job for a woman. But Agnes chose to fulfil both roles and in these windows motherhood is shown to be the driving force of her art. Thus the picture is a personal statement about the difficult task of balancing two roles.

The windows also tell a true and tragic story. Shortly before Agnes handed in the sketch, she lost her daughter who was just 4 months old. Motherhood can be as fragile as the glass on which it is painted.

COLLECTION OF MODELS AT CITY HALL

Copenhagen City Hall
Rådhuspladsen, 1599 K
• Access on Culture Night or by appointment with the Town Hall
Information office (tel: 33 66 25 84)
• S-train: Copenhagen Central Station

I f you book in advance, it is possible to climb to the attic of City Hall, which provides access to both the City Hall Tower and two surprising rooms containing an unexpected collection of full-scale models. Although the rooms were once open to the public (as the many meticulously carved visitors' names testify), visits are now by appointment only.

> *Why have a sphinx when you can have a polar bear?*

The stars of the collection are undoubtedly the two polar bears (the work of the sculptor Bundgaard), although the rooms are also full of models of the buildings' many other fanciful decorative elements, both interior and exterior. The two polar bear sculptures made from the models are perched discreetly on a ledge on the very top of the façade overlooking City Hall square.

When City Hall was built in 1905, there was much controversy about the two polar bears: numerous people preferred more conventional sculptures, such as lions or sphinxes. The architect, Martin Nyrop, was even called upon to defend his vision and his ideas – he explained, quite simply, that the bears were inspired by Denmark's connections with the Arctic.

City Hall, particularly the attic, houses a number of interesting attractions that are not included in the standard guided tours: for example, the old attic kitchen; the roof-top ledge offering a unique bird's eye view of the city; and the interior of Pigeon Tower. They can be visited under the same conditions as the collection of models.

AN ATMOSPHERIC FORMER BATHHOUSE

Hotel Ascot vestibule, formerly *Badeanstalten Kjøbenhavn*
Studiestræde 59–63, 1554 V
• S-train: Vesterport

When the Swedes taught Copenhagen to take a proper bath

I f you look up at the building in Studiestræde 59–63, the one right opposite the *Pumpehuset* (a former pumping station), you will see the word *Renlighed* (cleanliness) carved in big letters: the word testifies that this building, which now houses the Hotel Ascot, originally opened its doors as a bathhouse in 1903.

Back then, Copenhagen was densely populated and cleanliness was not a primary concern of the many people who lived in small, dark, and cramped apartments. To most people, taking a warm bath was something that happened only once a year. Hence, the bathhouses that appeared in the latter half of the 19th century and the beginning of the 20th were something of a revelation. Most of the staff at *Badeanstalten Kjøbenhavn* came from Sweden, where, over the course of time, a special culture of bathing had developed.

In the bathhouse, the main baths were situated in the middle and rear sections of the building. In the basement, there was a cheaper bath catering for the poorest of the city's inhabitants. The sign for this people's bath can still be seen above the door which leads down to the basement in one of the building's backyards.

If, on the other hand, you go through the main entrance into the vaulted vestibule of the hotel, you can sense that it was once a really special place: the room has beautiful panels made of cypress wood, and stucco decorations, which show children frolicking in the water.

Just off the vestibule, in what is today the hotel restaurant, is the former women's changing room. The men's section was on the first and second floors. Here, there were changing rooms, plunge tubs, bathtubs, shower rooms, massage rooms and rooms for manicures, as well as Roman and Russian–Finnish baths. One could also just sit down and relax in a wicker chair and play a game of dominoes, or enjoy a drink. The bathhouse also had medicinal baths. A particularly popular treatment was the Swedish *gyttja* massage bath where the Master of the Bath would rub a warm peat-like mud, filled with microscopic silicon, onto the skin of the guest. To counteract fatigue after such a treatment one had to rest for half an hour before slowly dressing and returning to the streets of Copenhagen.

PICTURE HALL IN GRUNDTVIG'S HOUSE ❺

Today home to KAB (Københavns Almene Boligselskab)
Studiestræde 36-40, 1455 K
• Access by appointment only
• S-train, Metro: Nørreport

> *Seventy-seven peasants, including a girl from the West Indies and another from Greenland*

Grundtvig's House is a strange and impressive building which, despite being easy to overlook in the narrow Studiestræde, is well worth a visit. The property is currently owned and run by the Copenhagen General Housing Association (KAB), which took it over in 1972. It was originally built, as the name implies, to honour N. F. S. Grundtvig (1783–1872), a famous and influential figure in Denmark.

Grundtvig was the founding father of the Danish Folk High School, and the house was used as a centre for the promulgation of his thoughts and ideas on Christian education.

The house is a fine example of the Danish national-romantic style of architecture. Its beautiful picture hall has a monumental mural covering three of its four walls, painted by Rudolf Rud-Petersen (1871–1961). The mural features a panorama of Danish folk history, with seventy-seven people from all over the Kingdom of Denmark preparing to hang a garland of flowers and foliage on the walls.

Most of the figures are Danish peasants dressed in regional costumes. When you go in, you'll see people from Seeland to your left, from Jutland on your right and from Funen on the wall behind you. But there's also a woman from Iceland, a man from the Faroe Islands and girls from Greenland and the former Danish West Indies. The West Indian girl is leaning against a door listening to a man playing a violin; next to her, a boy holds up the *Dannebrog*, the Danish flag.

WINDOW IN HESTEMØLLESTRÆDE

Hestemøllestræde 4, 1464 K
• S-train, Metro: Nørreport

A small opening onto the dramas of everyday life

I f you go down Slutterigade between the courthouse and the old prison and then turn left down Hestemøllestræde, heading for Vandkunsten, you will pass three arched windows at street level. In the last of these, one of the eight small glass panes can be opened from the street, allowing you to see into the basement and peek at a shaky-looking little metal shelf inside. It doesn't look like anything now but it used to be the repository of "hot" news. Until 1997 the basement was used by the Danish Press Bureau, which, since 1921, had made its money by providing legal records to the press, which, in turn, used the information as the basis of its many sensationalist stories. Reporters from the Bureau attended court hearings to record the proceedings of violent and shocking trials as the confessions and denials of wife beaters, thieves, arsonists and murderers were their meat and drink. In those days, the minutes of the trials, with their carbon copies, were typed out, ready to be dispatched to the various subscribers, all in differently coloured envelopes. *Politiken, Berlingske Tidende, Det Fri Aktuelt, Ekstra Bladet, BT* and the news agency Ritzau all received their daily diet of sensationalism in this way.

The envelopes were then stacked on the little shelf behind the window in the basement. From there, they were collected by the newspapers' messenger boys and delivered to the journalists, who then transformed the reports into dramatic tales of life's miseries. In 1997 it was decided that the courthouse could no longer accommodate the Danish Press Bureau, so the basement, with its quirky little window, soon went out of use.

FREDERIKSBORG STUFFED HORSE

The Royal Stables and Carriages Museum at Christiansborg Palace
Christiansborg Ridebane 12, 1218 K
• Open 1.30pm–4pm Tue–Sun
• Admission: child 20 DKK, adult 40 DKK
• S-train: Copenhagen Central Station

> **The horse that ran for a seat in the Kunstkammer**

When you walk into the Royal Stables from the riding arena behind the Christiansborg Palace, the first thing that greets you is the heavy, humid air and the smell of horses. This is where a handful of very enthusiastic people work to help keep these stables going. Now a shadow of their former self, the stables used to be the most important department in the Royal Palace. Two hundred and fifty years ago, when the building was new, the stables housed up to three hundred horses. Today, there are only fourteen left, plus one. This one, however, is quite dead: it is three hundred and thirty years old, and stuffed as well.

In the summer of 1684, the English ambassador, Robert Molesworth, visited the Royal Stables in Copenhagen. He was received by the Master of the Stables, von Haxthausen, who proudly boasted about his horses and, in particular, about how fast they were.

As a true Englishman, Molesworth could not leave without making a bet. The Master of the Stables insisted that all his horses could run the distance from Copenhagen to Hillerød in less than three quarters of an hour. Molesworth doubted this so much that, without hesitation, sensing a safe bet, he put up 1,000 Dutch ducats. The two gentlemen agreed the conditions: The Master of the Stables was to be allowed fourteen days to prepare for the race. This time was to be spent making the necessary arrangements so that the road between Copenhagen and Hillerød would be ready and hedges, fences and any other obstacles could be removed. In addition, the Master of the Stables himself was to choose the stable boy to ride the horse. If the young jockey succeeded, he was to receive a sum of 100 ducats as a reward, as well as a job for life. And finally, two clockmakers were called in to time the race, one to be located in Copenhagen, the other in Hillerød.

The race was run on the 9th August, and the whole city of Copenhagen, as well as the people from Hillerød, gathered to take part in the fun. And, of course, the horse didn't let them down. It ran the distance of forty kilometres in forty-two minutes, only to drop dead on reaching the Hillerød city gates. This exceptionally fast run accorded it great honour as well as a place in the king's *Kunstkammer* next to many other extraordinary animals.

THE MOORING RINGS IN THE LIBRARY GARDEN

The Royal Library Garden, Slotsholmen
Access from *Rigsdagsgården* or Christians Brygge
• Open all year from 6am–10pm
• Metro: Christianshavn, Kongens Nytorv

8

> *What is left of one of Europe's major warship harbours*

Directly opposite the busy main staircase that leads to the Danish Parliament there's a beautiful old building, which was originally the library and *Kunstkammer* of King Frederik III. Go through the gates, make your way through the building and you'll come to a hidden garden, where all the noise of the city vanishes. On a low brick wall at one end of the garden hang some rusty, but remarkable traces of the past: three old iron mooring rings which bear witness to the fact that this now peaceful place was once King Christian IV's noisy, bustling harbour from where his proud fleet of warships would set sail. In the 17th century it was the site of a large, square, four-metre-deep harbour, which could only be accessed from the coastline by means of a twenty-five-metre-long canal. Here, side by side, and hidden behind the massive wall of buildings which surrounded the harbour, lay the warships, moored to these old iron rings. From behind the water gates soldiers would load the ships with canons, armour from the armoury and foodstuffs from the warehouses.

During the reign of Christian IV, the Danish fleet grew to be one of the largest in Europe and the construction of the harbour, which took place between 1598 and 1611, was of fundamental importance to the Danes' attempts to maintain hegemony over the Baltic Sea. When it was finished, the armoury building was the largest of its kind in northern Europe. A German prince visiting the site reported how he saw endless rows of canons and armour there and that in the harbour he saw three hundred beautiful ships – and a white bear, which had

probably been brought to Copenhagen by one of the expeditions to Greenland.

With time, the harbour lost its importance, and, in 1867, it was filled in with enormous quantities of rubble. The abandoned area was first taken over by a gun manufacturer, and then, in 1920, the architect Thorvald Jørgensen designed the Library Garden.

THE MULBERRY TREE

East gable of *Proviantgården* on Slotsholmen
Access from Christians Brygge
• Metro: Christianshavn, Kongens Nytorv

> *Under the crown of the oldest mulberry tree in Denmark*

An ancient mulberry tree grows beside the east gable wall in the *Proviantgården*. The site itself does not attract much attention and the tree stands by itself near a car park where cars drive up and down the street and people pass by in a steady stream going in and out of the Library Garden.

If you see it from the car park, the mulberry tree just looks like a big untidy bush. However, if you enter the garden from behind the curtain of green branches you'll find yourself in a hidden world, which seems to be made of distorted tree trunks. The end of August is a good time to visit because then, the tree is covered in big juicy mulberries, which look rather like big blackberries, but, remember, if you pick them, they'll leave your fingers stained with red juice. According to the gardeners who have taken care of the tree for generations, the mulberry tree has a fascinating history. It is said to have grown from a seed that dropped out of a shipping crate at some point in the 17th century when the area was the harbour for King Christian IV's warships. Close to the wall in a sheltered location, the site apparently provided such good growing conditions that the tree has survived and is today considered to be Denmark's oldest mulberry tree. It's almost four hundred years old, but is also a very well-kept secret.

Mulberry trees have been grown in Denmark since the 1500s, and for centuries the juicy berries have been used for jams and other confectionery. But, when Denmark wanted to found its own silk industry in the 17th century, it was not the berries that were sought after, but the leaves: mulberry leaves are a natural food source for the silkworm, whose cocoons are used in the production of silk.

THE AURORA PAINTING

Den Stormske Gård, Ministry of Finance
Slotsholmsgade 8, 1216 K
• Open on Culture Night
• Metro: Kongens Nytorv

The King's Dawn

Slotsholmsgade is lined with a number of fine buildings, which today house the offices and meeting rooms of various government ministries, but it was not always so. The buildings were erected in the 17th century as stately homes for noblemen and merchants who wanted to be close to the nearby stock exchange. One of these houses, *Den Stormske Gård*, is named after an Icelandic merchant who built the house in 1696.

In one of the wings of the building, an 18th-century room is now used for meetings, but still retains its original features. Its walls are covered in reddish brown floral wallpaper and examples of 18th-century gilding are evident. There is also a balcony with a wooden balustrade, and a small hidden door, once used by servants as a secret passage which allowed them to go about their duties unobtrusively. The high point of the room, however, is the ceiling, which is beautifully painted using a *trompe-l'œil* effect, creating an illusion of looking up at a dome decorated with amorous figures.

Executed in 1712 by the court painter, Hendrik Krock, the painting depicts Dawn in the shape of the Roman goddess, Aurora, strewing flowers on the ground to welcome the dawning of the new day. The goddess is surrounded by cupids showing us that this day will be one dedicated to Love, that of King Frederik IV for a young lady.

To find out the story behind the painting, we need to look back into the reign of the Danish king, Frederik IV. In 1711 plague broke out in Copenhagen and people died like flies. King Frederik fled to Koldinghus in Jutland with his queen and court. The king was a man who loved pleasure and the first thing he did upon arriving in Jutland was to invite all the beautiful young girls from the local nobility to a masquerade. The very young Anna Sophie Reventlow, a daughter of the House of Clausholm, was one of those invited and the king immediately fell in love with her. A year later, the king abducted her and married her secretly, also known as marrying her to his "left hand".

Back home in Copenhagen, the king got rid of his old mistress and refurbished *Den Stormske Gård* for his new "wife" filling it with beautiful furniture and paintings. The house was conveniently located close to the palace, and, through a connecting walkway, the king could make his way directly to Anna Sophie's chambers without being seen. Anna Sophie lived in the house until 1721 when Frederik's queen died and Anna Sophie officially became the new Queen of Denmark.

THE STRUENSEE ROOM

Den Røde Bygning, Ministry of Finance
Christiansborg Slotsplads 1, 1218 K
• Open on Culture Night
• Metro: Kongens Nytorv

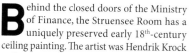

The other Struensee

Behind the closed doors of the Ministry of Finance, the Struensee Room has a uniquely preserved early 18th-century ceiling painting. The artist was Hendrik Krock and it depicts Justice and Peace kissing each other. Here, Krock was heavily influenced by the work of the Italian artist Girolamo Troppa, in the church of San Carlo al Corso in Rome. But the room, with its covering of dark wallpaper, also has a powerful and sinister appearance which is in keeping with the fate of the person whose room it once was.

For generations, it has been called the Struensee Room, but surprisingly, not after the famous German physician Johann Friedrich Struensee, who was one of the most powerful and notorious figures in 18th-century Denmark, but after Carl August Struensee (1735–1804), his much less well-known older brother.

Carl August was a professor, and taught mathematics, military science and philosophy. And even though he had no experience in financial administration, his brother persuaded him to come to Denmark to help manage the country's finances. C.A. Struensee had a great talent for organization and was behind some significant initiatives; he was, for example, the first person in the financial history of Denmark to set an overall budget for the Treasury.

But in January 1772 it all went wrong, and Carl August, along with his famous younger brother, was arrested and taken to the prison in the Citadel (see below). It was not until after the execution of Johann Friedrich that Carl August was released and sent back to Prussia. Before leaving, he signed a statement promising never to speak about the events in Denmark, a promise he kept.

JOHANN FRIEDRICH STRUENSEE (1737–1772)

In 1768, Johann Friedrich Struensee became the personal physician to the insane Danish monarch, King Christian VII. In 1769, Struensee moved to Copenhagen and was permanently attached to the court. In 1770 he overthrew the people behind the mad king and took power himself. He was behind a series of reforms in line with the ideals of the Enlightenment, but in January 1772, he fell victim to a coup and was found guilty of having an affair with Queen Caroline Mathilde. He was executed on 28 April 1772.

For the marble bathtub at Frederiksberg Palace and its connection to Struensee, see p.117.

THE STATUE OF ASCLEPIUS

Prins Jørgens Gård, 1218 K
• Metro: Kongens Nytorv

Thorvaldsen's blunder

The four impressive bronze sculptures in the courtyard of *Prins Jørgens Gård* should symbolise Courage, Wisdom, Justice and Truth. But because of a mistake by the renowned Danish sculptor Bertel Thorvaldsen (1770–1844), Health has replaced Truth.

Thorvaldsen was in Rome when he was chosen to design these statues. In a letter he received from Copenhagen instructing him to create four statues as allegories of the four royal virtues, Thorvaldsen mistakenly read "health" (*sundhed* in Danish) instead of "truth" (*sandhed*). So just because of the confusion between two vowels, the three famous figures of Hercules (Courage), Minerva (Wisdom) and Nemesis (Justice) strangely came to be accompanied by Asclepius (Latin Aesculapius), the Graeco-Roman god of healing and health.

Although Thorvaldsen was commissioned in 1810, no final agreement was signed until 1843. By that time the artist was growing old and had gone back to live in Denmark. He could no longer manage the tiring work of a sculptor and just managed to finish the statue of Hercules before his death in 1844. The job was completed by the sculptor H. W. Bissen, following Thorvaldsen's original sketches.

Why has this misunderstanding never been rectified? Over time, "Health" may be more thought-provoking than "Truth", as the representation of Asclepius was completed a few years before the insalubrious living conditions of Copenhagen led to a severe cholera epidemic in 1853, which killed almost 5,000 people.

Initially, the four sculptures were intended for the second Christiansborg Palace, which was built in the early 19th century but burned down in 1884. They were installed in four alcoves and on the façade of the palace. After the fire, the present Christiansborg Palace was built at the turn of the 20th century. The four sculptures were then transferred to *Prins Jørgens Gård*.

ELEPHANTS IN THE FORMER HEADQUARTERS ⓭ OF THE EAST ASIATIC COMPANY

Holbergsgade 2, 1057 K
- Open during normal office hours
- Metro: Kongens Nytorv

Elephants in a courtyard

At the corner of Holbergsgade and Niels Juels Gade, a large building contains some interesting modern architecture as well as an amusing reminder of Denmark's largest industrial adventure of the 20th century.

Today the building belongs to Danske Bank, but, even if you don't have an account with them, don't hesitate to ring the bell and you will be allowed to go inside its beautiful lobby. If you ask nicely, you may also be allowed to look at the large glass-covered courtyard, which is located in the middle of the building.

Formerly open to the skies (you can still see the outer windowsills), the courtyard is now a huge glass-covered area whose transparent roof extends to a height of six storeys. There's a rather flashy fountain with a golden globe, but the atmosphere here is quiet, almost meditative, even though it's in the middle of the bustling city centre.

On one wall, a narrow glass elevator travels up to the top of the building where – very surprisingly – two large elephants, carved from sandstone, overlook the courtyard. Now rather squashed by the elevator, which is clearly of a later date, the elephants are a relic from the period between 1908 and 1994 when the building was the headquarters of the East Asiatic Company (EAC). Much of the growth of the EAC was founded on the teak trade from Siam (now Thailand). EAC owned a large herd of elephants which were trained to work on the logging sites. Their job was to haul the timber through the jungle and then to load it onto the ships. It was then transported abroad, often ending up as home or garden furniture.

Today there is almost nothing left of the EAC: the sandstone elephants are the final reminders of a piece of Danish industrial history.

ERICHSEN'S HOUSE

Today home to Danske Bank
Holmens Kanal 2, 1060 K
• Access: keep an eye on the programme for Culture Night
• Metro: Kongens Nytorv

The Nereid on the back of a sea panther

The marvellous building known as Erichsen's House was built for the wealthy shipping agent Erich Erichsen in the late 1790s by the architect Caspar Frederik Harsdorff. In the first-floor corner room, facing Holmens Kanal, a rather erotic ceiling painting by the Hamburg-based company of Masson and Ramée created a sensation when it was unveiled in 1800.

The painting shows a Nereid (tasked by the Greek gods with protecting seafarers) portrayed as a beautiful, voluptuous woman draped over the back of a strange and fabulous leopard-like creature boasting both wings and the tail of a fish.

The Copenhagen *Nereid and the Sea Panther* is in fact a copy of a Roman wall painting found in the 18th century at Stabiae, a small town near Pompeii and Herculaneum that had also been destroyed in the volcanic eruption of Vesuvius in A.D. 79. In the 18th century it was all the rage to have homes decorated in the "Pompeian style", as the well-to-do were enthralled by recent discoveries made during the excavations in Southern Italy.

Looking up at the ceiling, the maritime theme continues in the form of a painted garland of 200 conch shells that encircles the room: shell and curio collecting was very popular with the wealthier classes at that time.

HER GIEMMES LEVNINGEN
AF
IORDANO
ET MYNSTER PAA TROSKAB
HAN BLEV FODT I ROM
I PII SEXTI REGIERINGS
ANDET AAR
HAN DODE I KIOBENHAVN
I DET MERKELIGE AAR
DA ET PUND SUKKER
STOE ALIII SKILL

SCULPTORS' GARDEN

Behind Charlottenborg Palace, Kongens Nytorv 1, 1051 K
• Access: ask the Academy of Fine Arts warden whose office is situated in the main building facing Kongens Nytorv
• Metro: Kongens Nytorv

I n summer, one of the most delightful places to visit in Copenhagen is the Sculptors' Garden, hidden away in the furthermost courtyard of the Charlottenborg Palace, towards Heibergsgade. The garden and its studios serve as workspaces for students studying sculpture at the Academy of Fine Arts.

The faithful dog and the enchanted garden

Among the plants are vestiges of the university's third Botanical Garden, which was situated here from the 1770s to the 1880s, as well as broken pieces of stone capitals and columns – remains of C. F. Hansen's second Christiansborg Palace, destroyed by fire in 1884.

In the centre of the garden stands a rather unusual tombstone whose inscription tells a story of touching devotion and loyalty. It reads:

HERE LIE THE RELICS OF [G]IORDANO, A TRUE EXAMPLE OF LOYALTY. HE WAS BORN IN ROME IN THE SECOND YEAR OF THE REIGN OF POPE PIUS THE SIXTH. HE DIED IN COPENHAGEN [IN] THAT STRANGE YEAR WHEN A POUND OF SUGAR COST XLIII SKILLING.

Giordano was actually a dog owned by the painter and architect Nicolai Abildgaard (1743–1809): he was his master's faithful companion from their first meeting in Italy some time in the mid-1770s until he was laid to rest in the garden behind the Charlottenborg in the early 1790s.

One night, on a trip down the River Po, Giordano began to behave strangely and, early next morning, he jumped overboard and swam to the shore to relieve himself. Afterwards, the dog tried to swim back on board but the current in the river was too strong. He tried and tried but eventually had to give up and the boat left without him. Crestfallen, Giordano sat on the bank watching it slowly disappear. But he soon rallied and started chasing it along the riverbank. Abildgaard himself, in recollecting the event, said he had given up hope of ever seeing his dog again, but later the same day, the faithful Giordano caught up with the boat, found a shallow place in the river, threw himself into the water and swam to be reunited with his master!

The tombstone in the garden today is a reproduction of the original stone, which is now safely stored away to protect it from the Danish weather.

PANEL OF SMOKING ANGELS

⓰

The former Hirschsprung tobacco shop
Strøget, Østergade 6, 1100 K
• Metro: Kongens Nytorv

> **When even angels smoked a pipe of tobacco**

The door of Østergade 6 is decorated with a charming cast iron panel whose subject might well raise eyebrows today. In the midst of its entwined (tobacco) plants sit three little winged boys, all intently indulging in the pleasures of tobacco. One is standing smoking a long, elegant pipe. Another is enjoying a cigar, which he holds in his left hand while he clutches an entire bundle for later use in his right. Sitting in the centre with his eyes turned heavenwards, the third little angel holds a small snuffbox in one hand as he helps himself to a pinch with the other.

The door dates from around 1870 when the Hirschsprung tobacco manufacturers (brothers Bernhard and Heinrich Hirschsprung) opened a new modern retail business on the site. The Hirschsprung firm was originally founded in 1826 by their father, Abraham Marcus Hirschsprung, a German–Jewish immigrant. However, in 1859 the brothers took over the company, and it was largely due to their success in business that they were able to form the basis for their great art collection, which was gifted to the Danish state in 1902 and which, by 1911, was on display to the public in the museum in the Østre Anlæg.

Why is there no cigarette-smoking angel on the panel though? What needs to be borne in mind is that the Danes didn't take to machine-rolled tobacco until the late 1800s and, in fact, cigarette smoking didn't really become popular until – in the wake of the Second World War – it acted as a symbol of freedom. Pipe smoking, however, was actually the first way in which tobacco was enjoyed when it was introduced in the 17th century. Snuff tobacco, in turn, was a fashion phenomenon belonging firmly to the 18th. Cigars only came into vogue in the middle of the 19th century when they were regarded as a more practical alternative to a pipe: a cigar could be carried anywhere and it could easily be enjoyed both at home and on the street.

THE PATERNOSTER LIFT

Belysningsvæsenet building (now the KVUC)
Vognmagergade 53, 1120 K
• Open weekdays from morning until evening throughout the school year
• S-train: Nørreport, Metro: Nørreport, Kongens Nytorv

A round trip?

If you want to experience perpetual motion you should try a little joyride on one of Copenhagen's five paternoster lifts. You'll find they are rather different from the lifts or elevators you're used to. Three of them are still easily accessible and the one in a building in the Vognmagergade is probably the best to try. It's quite small, but still fun to have a go on. It's also free and can be a great place to get into conversation with other visitors.

The lift is the same age as the building, which was completed in 1913, and its rather old technology makes for an unusual experience. The paternoster consists of open cabins which run without stopping, so take your time, take a deep breath, jump into the next one that comes level with you and off you go! Take a few trips round and experience the sensation of being inside the mechanical heart of an old building. Probably the best known of these lifts is the one in the Danish parliament building. Most Danes remember the televised images of one of their elected politicians fleeing the press by jumping into the Parliament paternoster. Whilst all five lifts still exist at present (see below), they are not getting any younger and may go out of use, so, if you want to experience perpetual motion, hurry up before it's too late!

THE FIVE PATERNOSTERS OF COPENHAGEN

If you are interested in tracking down all five of the lifts the first can be found in the *Belysningsvæsenet* (now the KVUC) as described above. The second is a quite well-preserved one in the Axelborg building opposite the main entrance to the Tivoli Gardens. The third, which is very accessible, is located in the Frederiksberg City Hall. This one, which can be visited during normal office hours, is relatively recent as the hall was only built in the 1940s. The final two, the one in the Christiansborg Palace (the Parliament paternoster as described above), and the one in the Danske Bank headquarters in Holmen's Kanal, are not accessible to the public.

WHERE DOES THE NAME 'PATERNOSTER' COME FROM?

The action of the loop system through which the cabins move, passing endlessly on rotating chains, reminded someone of the movement of rosary beads clicking while the Lord's Prayer (Pater Noster in Latin) was being recited.

WHEN WERE THE PATERNOSTERS INVENTED?

They date from 1877 when they were invented by Frederick Hart. The very first one was installed in Kent in the south of England.

The lifts were popular at first because they could take more people and were faster than other types of lift. However, safety considerations killed off most of the paternosters and there are very few left now.

Those that remain are regarded as interesting antiques which are still fun to use.

QUEEN'S BOX AT THE REFORMED CHURCH

Reformed Church, Gothersgade 111, 1123 K
• Open during Sunday services from 10am
• S-train, Metro: Nørreport

*A real
time warp*

I n Gothersgade, directly opposite Rosenborg Castle, the Reformed church – home to German, French and Korean congregations – is a world of beautiful carved woodwork. The walls are a stark white and the interior is devoid of any religious imagery. There are none of the altar paintings or crucifixes that are to be found in the Danish National Church, as the Protestant Reformed Church disapproved of pictorial decoration in its churches.

From the small entrance area just inside the church, a narrow staircase leads to a gallery where there is an octagonal box with a crown on top and sides made of panes of glass. This encloses an odd little room with angels painted on the ceiling, containing an old Baroque chair hemmed in by walls made of blue-marbled wooden panels covered in gold tooled leather. A real time warp.

Called the Queen's Box, it was built as a tribute to the German-born Queen Charlotte Amalie, who followed the Reformed faith and who, in 1667, married King Christian V. Prior to the marriage, her father made it a condition that she be allowed to keep her faith. In 1689, her husband built a Reformed church on Gothersgade, the first place in which the Reformed congregation could practise their religion. However, the building burned down during the Great Copenhagen Fire of 1728 and, in 1731, the church was rebuilt largely in the style of its predecessor. Although the queen had been dead for sixteen years, a new Queen's Box was built in a similar style to the original.

HORSE AND LION SCULPTURE

The King's Garden (Kongens Have)
Gothersgade, 1123 K
• Open all year from sunrise to sunset
• S-train: Nørreport, Metro: Kongens Nytorv, Nørreport

Lion with a human face

I f you walk along the Kavalergangen in the King's Garden, parallel to Gothersgade, you can't miss *The Horse and the Lion* sculpture. It is not only the oldest statue in the garden, and the oldest public sculpture in Copenhagen, but also probably the only one in Denmark depicting a lion with a human face and a centre parting in his mane.

The Horse and the Lion is a copy of one of the most famous statues of antiquity which, over the centuries, has taken many guises. The original, which can be seen today in Rome's Capitoline Museums, dates back to the time of Alexander the Great. When the Roman Empire dominated the world, the statue was brought back to Rome as a war trophy, then became a symbol of Justice in the Middle Ages. During the Renaissance it was admired and praised for its artistic qualities, which is why King Christian IV commissioned a replica – perhaps without knowing exactly what he intended to do with it.

There are several indications that producing this statue was an almost impossible feat: the casts of the two animals and the last section of gilding were not completed until 1624, eight years after work began. It is not clear where the sculpture was placed at first, but legend has it that Christian IV commissioned it to commemorate his defeat at the Battle of Lutter am Barenberg, during the Thirty Years War. Before the battle began, an ally of the Danish king, George Duke of Brunswick-Lüneburg, suddenly deserted him in favour of the Catholic League.

The big cat was therefore meant to symbolise the heroic lion of the North taking its revenge on the traitor, the horse of Lüneburg, grasped in its jaws. However as the Battle of Lutter took place in 1626, two years after the sculpture was completed, this story cannot be entirely accurate.

Nevertheless, there is evidence that from 1626 onwards the sculpture was the subject of much political debate. In Copenhagen, after the Battle of Lutter, coins were in circulation featuring a lion tearing the skin off a horse on one side, and on the other a Latin inscription recalling the honourable lion's hatred of traitors who don't keep their word.

GUD · HALLELUJA · SALIGGIØRELSE · OG · ÆRE · OG · PRI

HERREN · ER · MIN · HYRDE · MIG · SKAL · INTET · FATTES

CHURCH AT THE *KOMMUNEHOSPITALET*

Centre for Health and Society, University of Copenhagen
Øster Farimagsgade 5, 1353 K
• Access only by prior arrangement with the property group, Jeudan
(tel: 39 11 92 25)
• S-train, Metro: Nørreport

A hidden gem under the dome

Locked and hidden away like a time capsule, the church at the former Municipal Hospital (*Kommunehospitalet*) is a real gem. Unfortunately, it has hardly ever been open to the public since the hospital closed in the late 1990s. To gain access, it is necessary to make a special arrangement with the building's new owners, the property group, Jeudan.

On sunny days, the church is lit by a magical light which streams in through the windows, bathing the little altar in a red glow. In the lunette above the altar, Christ sits with two angels by his side. In the south aisle, there is an illustration of the congregation accepting the words and wisdom of Christ in the form of a cross surrounded by a flock of sheep drinking from a well.

The church decoration is inspired by Greek and Byzantine architecture. The hospital's architect, Hans Christian Hansen, had lived in Greece between 1833 and 1849. He then travelled extensively before returning to Copenhagen in 1857; one of his first assignments there was to build the *Kommunehospitalet*.

The façade, with its pattern of nine layers of yellow bricks and three layers of red, is a reference to the wall built by the Byzantine Emperor Theodosius II around the city of Constantinople (Istanbul). When the hospital was completed in 1863, the church interior was still undecorated. It took another thirty years before the matter was addressed, using the Byzantine features of Hansen's original design. Both the decoration of the lunettes, and the dark blue sky strewn with golden stars, were inspired by Byzantium.

The *Kommunehospitalet* was built in response to the great cholera epidemic of 1853: Copenhagen desperately needed the clean air from the other side of the city ramparts and, perhaps even more urgently, it needed a modern hospital. By the standards of the day, the new hospital was huge, with its 800 beds; it also had boilers, ventilation rooms, laundry facilities and a stable, as well as a place for carriages. And, very importantly, it had little gardens where convalescent patients could enjoy fresh air and sunlight in a pleasant environment.

ROSENBORG BASTION

Øster Voldgade 3, 1350 K
The bastion is part of the Botanical Garden
• The Astronomical Observatory is normally open on Culture Night
• S-train, Metro: Nørreport

*Honouring
Tycho Brahe*

Tycho Brahe (1546–1601), the famous Danish astronomer, had a fascinating life and you'll find a sort of unofficial monument to him on a hill called the Rosenborg Bastion. It's in a corner of the Botanical Garden and when you climb up you'll also have a wonderful view out over Copenhagen. The hill itself is dominated by two closely related monuments: the Astronomical Observatory designed by Christian Hansen and a statue of Tycho Brahe by the sculptor Herman Wilhelm Bissen.

Built between 1859 and 1861, the observatory consists of a central tower surrounded by two lateral pavilions: the one to the east was originally home to the professor of astronomy and the one to the west was the home of the observer himself. But the most impressive feature is not visible: in order to completely eliminate vibrations of the lens telescope (the refractor), the observatory tower is embedded in foundations which run underneath the entire building until they reach street level. One third of all the bricks laid in the construction of the building were used in its foundations. To this day, a rotating dome fitted with hatches protects the telescope from bad weather. In 1895 the original telescope, which dated from 1861, was replaced by a new one which is still in place today.

On the exterior of the building, below the windows, you'll find some symbols which refer to Tycho's work in the field of astronomy. The two squares superimposed around a circle resemble those that he used symbolically to join Earth and Heaven when laying out his garden on the island of Hven - the square symbolized Earth and the circle, Heaven.

The statue of Tycho Brahe on the Rosenborg Bastion, however, was not erected until 1876. It shows the world-renowned astronomer standing looking out over the city. To his right is the old Round Tower Observatory, built in the 1630s by King Christian IV whose Rosenborg Castle is located right at Tycho's feet.

WAS TYCHO BRAHE THE FATHER OF CHRISTIAN IV AND A SOURCE FOR SHAKESPEARE'S *HAMLET*?

Tycho Brahe lived on the island of Hven from 1576 to 1596. Here, in the middle of the Øresund, he ran a small research centre that attracted massive financial support from King Frederik II. But just as things were going well for him at court, Tycho's patron, Frederik II, died and his son Christian IV came to the throne. Tycho was soon forced to look for a new patron – he found him in Prague, where Emperor Rudolf II was pleased to receive him.

However, no sooner had Tycho arrived in Prague than he died in October 1601. His death, and the circumstances surrounding it, have led to much speculation: is the story about him dying from a burst bladder true or was his death due to something more sinister? Tycho had lost part of his nose in a duel and for the rest of his life he wore a prosthetic nose. This fake nose was made from various metals, perhaps including mercury, which could have poisoned him. But the mystery remains unsolved as other factors in his colourful life lead some people to believe that he may have been deliberately poisoned.

Several historians are convinced that a crime was committed and many theories have been put forward. In January 2009, however, a new theory was presented. According to this, a distant relative of Tycho Brahe's, a man named Eric Brahe, was hired by none other than King Christian IV to murder Tycho. Because of his family ties, Eric stood a better chance of getting close to the famous astronomer. And in fact, Eric was with Tycho in the days leading up to his death and on the very day of his death.

Allegedly, Eric's motive for the killing was that he desperately needed the protection of a powerful sovereign because he had many enemies. And Christian IV's motive? One theory is that the self-glorifying king was simply jealous of Tycho and therefore wanted to get rid of him. A second theory is more complicated: Tycho, in the days of his youth, was said to have had an affair with Christian IV's mother, Queen Sophie. If the rumour was correct, Christian IV was the consequence of the affair: Tycho was not only Christian's father, but it also made Christian illegitimate, which nullified his claim to the throne.

According to the man behind this controversial theory, the historian Peter Hvilshøj Andersen, the story does not end here. After Tycho's mysterious death in Prague, the rumours swept across Europe and Shakespeare himself used them as inspiration for his play, *Hamlet*. The play is about the Prince of Denmark, Hamlet (alias Christian IV), who, in a dream, meets his father's ghost (alias Frederik II). His father tells Hamlet that it was his brother, Claudius (alias Tycho Brahe), who killed him. After this, Claudius lives on, sharing the throne with the widowed queen, Hamlet's mother, Gertrude (alias Queen Sophie). During the meeting with his father's ghost, Hamlet promises to seek revenge and kill Claudius.

Thus, if you are willing to equate Tycho's fate with Shakespeare's play, the brotherly bond between Hamlet's father (Frederik II) and Claudius (Tycho) must be seen as a spiritual connection rather than a physical one; and the "throne" that Claudius shares with Gertrude (Queen Sophie) should not be taken literally, but rather as the path to fame and glory trodden by Tycho.

If you are confused, it's probably nothing compared to Hamlet's confusion … or was it that of Christian IV?

CRAFTSMEN'S FRIEZE

㉒

Store Kongensgade 67, 1264 K
• Metro: Kongens Nytorv

> ### *The frieze with the busy apprentices*

There's a very fine frieze on both sides of the entrance to the house at Store Kongensgade 67, which could easily go unnoticed. It depicts eight hardworking young apprentices slaving away merrily for the former owner of the house, Peter Johannes Kretz. Kretz was himself a skilled craftsman – a cabinetmaker, plumber and engineer.

The boys, one for each of the house's eight bays, appear entwined in the tendrils of a vine from which hang small bunches of grapes. To your left, the first group of four boys represent Kretz's skill as a cabinetmaker. The first boy is handling a giant saw, the next holds a drill, the third apprentice is wielding

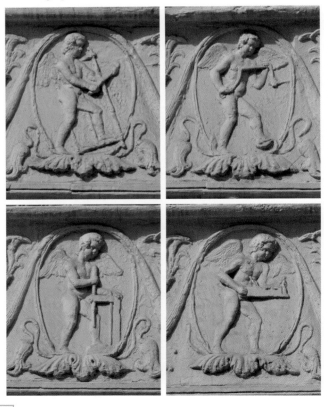

a large clamp and the last young craftsman is diligently working with a plane. The tools held by the boys to the right of the gate are a little harder to identify, but may refer to Kretz's other professions as engineer and plumber. In this part of the frieze, the first boy holds something that could be an old spirit level and the second is busy forging some kind of pipe, while the one next to him holds a pair of metal snips and a hammer. Finally, the last little fellow proudly displays a protractor and a set square.

Modelled in white painted stucco, the frieze was created by the architect Theophilus Hansen (1813–91) when he was a young student in Copenhagen, although it may be Kretz's own son, the sculptor P. J. Kretz Junior, who executed it. Theophilus designed it in 1837 when he was only 23 years old. The following year he left Copenhagen and went on a journey which led to him becoming one of the most influential architects of his day.

He became particularly famous in Vienna, where, among other buildings, he designed the famous Concert Hall, the Vienna *Musikverein*, and also the city's parliament.

PANORAMA FROM THE *PALAIS* GARAGES

Dronningens Tværgade 4, 1302 K
• Metro: Kongens Nytorv

Unknown to many Copenhageners, the garage in Dronningens Tværgade 4 offers a wonderful panoramic view of the city. To see it, go to the back of the building, walk past the petrol pump to the elevator which leads to the roof and have a look out over the city laid out before you. Up here, you'll be so close to the dome of the

With the dome of the Marble Church within reach

Marble Church that you could almost reach out and touch it.

On the way down, take the ramp and enjoy the experience of seeing Copenhagen's first multi-storey garage. Called the *Palais* Garages, they were built in two stages in 1932 and 1937 by the engineers Højgaard & Schultz, based on a design by the architect Oscar Gundlach-Pedersen (1886–1960).

The growth of car traffic in the 1930s resulted in increasingly heated debates about what to do with all these cars. Architects at the time were strongly influenced by the approach adopted in the US, where the multi-storey car park seemed to be the solution. But, at the same time, there was a certain nervousness in Copenhagen at the idea of allowing so many cars so close to one of the city's oldest and most distinguished buildings, Moltke's *Palais*.

In the passionate debate that followed, modern architects did all they could to convince the public that a car posed no threat to anyone or anything when it was standing in a garage.

In order to meet the concerns of the authorities – and also the neighbours – a vast range of security measures was installed, such as a modern sprinkler system and remote-controlled fire doors. The profitability of the garage was also dependent on the income from a service station located in the basement. Here, cars could be washed in ten to fifteen minutes in a semi-automatic plant, which could service sixty vehicles an hour. As the price of a wash also included chassis lubrication and air-drying, as well as a wipe-down, polish and vacuuming, the cars all benefited from a very thorough valet service.

While waiting, car owners could use the room on the ground floor, which was equipped with a telephone, a toilet and vending machines dispensing beer, soft drinks and sandwiches. They could then sit back and enjoy the view of the car wash through the plate-glass windows until loudspeakers informed them that their vehicle was ready. None of this remains today.

REJECTION FENCES AT AMALIENBORG

Behind the Harsdorff Colonnade
Amaliegade, 1256 K
• Metro: Kongens Nytorv

The magical influence of corners

In Amalienborg Palace Square, where Christian VII's Palace (which today serves as a residence for guests during state visits) and Christian IX's Palace (the Queen's winter residence) meet, if you walk from the square through the colonnade you'll see cast iron fences surmounted by spikes both on the left and right hand sides. These are the so-called 'rejection fences', designed to prevent people urinating in the corners.

The 'rejection fences' at the site today are not nearly as old as the problem they represent. The four Amalienborg palaces were built in the 1750s, while the colonnade, which was built in 1794 as a secret passageway between the king's palace and that of his son, enabled the royal family to move easily from one palace to another, but also created two corners perfectly suited to the need to pee.

Periodically, the misuse of the corners provoked outraged comments in the newspapers of the day and in the late 1830s these complaints became more and more frequent. It was said that no 'real' lady was in a position to use the street, not just because of the mess and smell, but also because of the likely risk that she would witness an unconcerned male standing in the corner urinating – often one of the palace guards. At one point, it was suggested that urinating at or in the vicinity of royal premises should be prohibited, as was the case in Sweden.

In the second half of the 19th century the two corners were equipped with urinals; the 'rejection fences' on the site today probably date from around 1900.

CHANDELIERS AT THE OPERA HOUSE

Access from Amaliehaven, 1253 K
• Metro: Kongens Nytorv

> **Hey, isn't that the Christiania logo?**

One evening, try sitting down by the waterfront at Amaliehaven and taking a closer look at Henning Larsen's Opera House, which is just across the water. Now imagine the foyer of the Opera House with its three enormous chandeliers hanging from the ceiling.

The light from the chandeliers, shining through the glass façade of the building, casts three huge yellow spots of light which stand out clearly against the dark red background.

You may not realise it at first, but look again and you will be in no doubt that, at night, the light cast by the chandeliers in the Opera House represents the three yellow "dots" which form the three letter "i"s in the word "Christiania", Copenhagen's self-proclaimed autonomous neighbourhood. So you are actually looking across the water at the Christiana logo: three yellow dots on a red background, writ large across the front of the Opera House.

We don't know for certain whether the Danish-Icelandic artist, Olafur Eliasson, who made the beautiful chandeliers, intended this as a whimsical reference to the logo, but it's a nice idea if he did.

ICON OF *MOTHER OF GOD OF JERUSALEM* ㉖

Aleksander Nevsky Church
Bredgade 53, 1260 K
• Open during worship and on vigil nights (see www.ruskirke.dk)
• Metro: Kongens Nytorv

> *A miracle
> right in
> the backyard*

The only Christian Orthodox church in Denmark, the Russian church in Bredgade has a number of icons on the first floor. The *Mother of God of Jerusalem* is the first icon that believers stop at when they enter the church.

On 10 March 1995, the first Friday of the Orthodox Church Great Fast, the icon began to weep tears. The following Sunday, and in the weeks that followed, this was repeated. The phenomenon only ceased with the coming of autumn. However, the following year, once again coinciding with the time of the Great Fast, the tears returned. The miracle inevitably attracted a lot of attention from the congregation of the Russian church, but, although it was so close to home, it aroused no interest in the wider Copenhagen public. Today, if you look closely, traces of the tears are still visible on the Madonna's cheeks.

The *Mother of God of Jerusalem* was supposedly painted in 1912 by a Russian monk. In 1928 it was given as a gift to the Danish-born Russian Empress Maria Feodorovna after her enforced return to Denmark following the Russian Revolution.

CHURCH AND EMPRESS

Dedicated to Alexander Nevsky, the Russian national hero and patron saint, the Russian church in Copenhagen was inaugurated in September 1883. The building was designed by the Russian architect David Ivanovich Grimm. However, according to legend, the Russian Tsar, who was present, was so displeased by the location of the building and its size that the inauguration ceremonies could not be performed as planned.

When the Danish Princess Dagmar married Tsar Alexander III in 1866, she converted to the Russian Orthodox faith and changed her name to Maria Feodorovna. Their eldest son, Nicholas II, became Russia's last Tsar. In 1918, with the October Revolution and the Bolsheviks' seizure of power, he was executed, along with his wife and children, in a cellar in Ekaterinburg. However, Maria Feodorovna did not leave Russia until the spring of 1919: she refused to accept that her son and his family had been murdered and, for a long time, believed that he had been rescued by a miracle. She died in the autumn of 1928 shortly after receiving the icon of the Holy Mother of God of Jerusalem, given to her to comfort her in all her sorrows.

APARTMENT IN THE NYBODER MUSEUM

Sankt Paulsgade 24, 1313 K
- www.nybodersmindestuer.dk
- Open Sun 11am-2pm
- Admission: child 10 DKK, adult 15 DKK
- S-train: Østerport

> *When children had to sleep in dresser drawers!*

All the locals know Nyboder, with its low orange-yellow buildings, a small "city within the city", which is still home to many naval personnel. However, very few outsiders know that one of Christian IV's original 17th-century houses still exists there. Since 1931, this house has been home to a small museum which tells the history of Nyboder. Run solely by volunteers, it is one of Copenhagen's smallest museums … and definitely the cosiest!

The main attraction is the Nyboder apartment, furnished as it was well into the 1900s. With its original furniture and fittings, it gives a wonderful sense of what life was like for the families who lived there. You'll ask yourself how up to twenty people managed in such cramped conditions, where the youngest children had to sleep in dresser drawers!

Be sure to mind your head when you go in as people in the 1600s were generally rather shorter than we are today. The apartment, in fact, seems like an enlarged doll's house, with room for everything, but all on a much smaller scale. It consists of a kitchen, a living room, two small bedrooms, a hall and another two small rooms in the attic.

The little kitchen, with its red and white checked curtains, gives a particularly good idea of the lack of space, as it is crammed full with an old stove, enamelled kitchenware and overcrowded plate racks. In many ways the heart of the home, the kitchen was where the women cooked and the girls were put to work cleaning the house. As there was no bathroom, it was also the only place where people could wash. But the kitchen was important for other reasons too because the family had to go through it to get to the courtyard, whether to drop off rubbish, hang out the washing or pay a visit to the outside toilet. As late as the 1930s, these houses only had a toilet in the courtyard.

The households would have been run by women because the men were often away at sea for long periods of time, but there was apparently a real community spirit. Elderly people who grew up in Nyboder say that it was common to care for each other and to help bring up each other's children. The upbringing was strict and the children were taught to be considerate towards others – a necessity when people were living in such close conditions.

THE NAVY'S SCHOOL FOR GIRLS

Today *Bygningskulturens Hus*
Borgergade 111, 1300 K
• www.bygningskulturenshus.dk
• Open during normal office hours
• S-train: Østerport

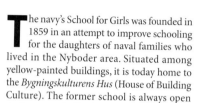

*For girls
in a world
of men*

T he navy's School for Girls was founded in
1859 in an attempt to improve schooling
for the daughters of naval families who
lived in the Nyboder area. Situated among
yellow-painted buildings, it is today home to
the *Bygningskulturens Hus* (House of Building
Culture). The former school is always open
during normal office hours, so you can just ask to look around.

The interior of the building is like a church, with a nave, two aisles and a
gallery. Its highlight is the central hall, where skylights allow the sunlight to
flood into the rooms. The carvings on the wooden beams in the roof and the
gallery were probably done by the navy's carpenters.

A staircase at the main entrance takes you up to the gallery. The staircase
walls are not whitewashed like those in the hall, but have been left in their
original unplastered state, revealing the grey and yellow masonry. This
"plainness" was exactly what the architects had been taught at the Academy of
Fine Arts – that, in the service of good taste, the best, and most honest, way to
handle materials was to leave them in as simple or "pure" a state as possible.

Built in 1859, the school was designed for 450 girls aged between 6 and 14.
But the architect, Bernhard Seidelin, came in for some harsh criticism. The
biggest outcry was probably over the placing of a communal latrine under
the stairs leading to the gallery. This facility consisted of a line of eight seats,
which were just holes drilled in a plank of wood for the use of all the girls. The
result was an intolerable stench which permeated the whole building. These
insanitary conditions were all the more serious as, in 1853, Copenhagen had
experienced its great cholera epidemic. Fortunately, the blunder was quickly
rectified and new latrines were built in the courtyard. The school was, however,
closed only ten years later, and from 1869 to 1939 it functioned as a naval
academy or cadet school. Between 1950 and 1970 it was the headquarters of
Naval Command.

BUNKER UNDER NYBODER SCHOOL

Nyboder Skole, Øster Voldgade 15, 1350 K
• Access can be difficult, but try contacting the Copenhagen Fire Brigade
(Københavns Brandvæsen): tel. 33 43 14 54
• S-train: Østerport

> *What a sports pitch might be hiding*

U nder Nyboder School lies a well-kept secret, unknown even to most of the parents whose children are pupils there. Today, it is the site of the indoor arena and sports pitch, but in 1941 and 1942 the occupying German army built a 740-m² bunker as a communications centre from where they could keep in touch with other strategic centres in Denmark. Later, during the Cold War, the bunker was turned into a command centre by the Civil Protection Organisation for use in the event of a nuclear attack – its official function until 1997.

Access to the bunker is by way of a small red brick building right next to the sports pitch. A staircase, which can be found behind a massive locked iron door, leads 5 m underground into the large reinforced concrete bunker. However, following severe water damage, it is now seriously threatened by damp and mould, and the atmosphere in the dank, shadowy bunker is rather eerie.

The bunker is divided into approximately 20 rooms, interconnected via a system of narrow corridors equipped with a row of glaring lamps. Down here, the smell of damp soil pervades the air and, as you move through the corridors, the cold air slowly catches up with you. You will pass machine and equipment rooms as well as a room sealed against a gas attack. There is also a communications room where old telephones still stand, surrounded only by mouldy chairs and torn telephone cables sticking out of holes in the walls. For a few years, some of the rooms functioned as a youth club, but when it closed, nobody bothered to clean up, and the place is littered with discarded sofas and boxes of old computer games.

The most fascinating area is the operations rooms where the work tables still stand, facing a giant map of Copenhagen. These are the rooms which, in 1952, were fitted out to serve as a command centre in the event of a nuclear attack. From here, emergency situations throughout Copenhagen were to be monitored. Behind the map there is a narrow aisle which allowed assistants to monitor the positions of the emergency services. This was done by moving small coloured markers around on the map to indicate the position of a fire engine or ambulance, for example.

SOUND HOLES OF KASTELSKIRKEN

Kastellet 15, 2100 Ø
- Access: the church is normally open on Sundays for worship, but the rest of the building can only be visited by special appointment with the Kastellets Venner association
- www.kastelletsvenner.dk
- S-train: Østerport

A strange sound system

At first glance, Kastelskirken Church, which was built in 1704, is a typical example of Danish Baroque style. However, the red building dating from 1725 and standing behind the church has some rather unusual architectural details, known as "sound holes".

The church was built within the military area of the citadel and, until the early 20th century, it catered exclusively to the military personnel and their families. The red building was for the inmates known as "prisoners of rank": either army officers or "state prisoners", those who were considered a risk to King and State.

However, Christian charity demanded that prisoners not be deprived of God's word, so a large number of holes were drilled in the church wall to enable the priest's voice to be heard. You can see this line of sound holes all along the western wall on the inside of the church. On the other side of the wall, inside the prison building, the holes line a narrow corridor linking the church to the prison cells. Sliding doors allowed the corridor to be divided into smaller sections, one for each cell. During worship, the prisoners were led from their cells and out into the corridor; the sliding doors were then pulled to and locked to prevent any contact between the prisoners.

For some prisoners, a stay in this building was the final stop before execution. This was the case for two prominent prisoners: the German-born Johann Friedrich Struensee and his henchman Enevold Brandt, who, in 1772, were both sentenced to death for *lèse-majesté*.

Two other notable prisoners were the so-called "Negro King" and his minister – two tribal chiefs who, in the late 1840s, were sent from the Danish colony on the African Gold Coast (approximately today's Ghana) to Copenhagen in order to serve their sentences. The two chiefs had been captured after sacrificing two of their enemies' children. They were finally sent home again after the colony was sold in 1850.

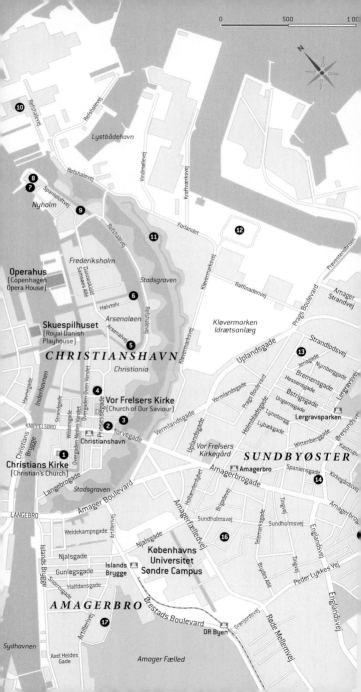

SOUTH

LINK WRAY'S GRAVE

Crypt of Christian's Church, Strandstræde 1, 1401 K
• Access: it is advisable to book a tour with the vicar (tel: 21 65 23 60)
• Open Tues–Fri 10am–4pm, and during regular church services
• Metro: Christianshavn

The guitar legend in the crypt

I n the crypt of Christian's Church lie the remains of the American guitar legend Fred Lincoln Wray (1929–2005), more widely known as "Link" Wray. Younger generations will know of him thanks to the soundtrack for the 1994 movie *Pulp Fiction*, while older generations might remember when, in 1958, he released his notorious single, "Rumble".

"Rumble" became one of the few instrumental tracks ever to be banned on American radio for fear that it would incite gang violence. Indeed, among other things, Link Wray was one of the musicians who inspired punk, metal and grunge music. At an early age, he was taught to play slide guitar and he is generally considered a pioneer in the development of the technique of distortion. As a sign of how influential "Rumble" is now considered to be, in 2008 it was selected to feature in the National Recording Registry at the Library of Congress. Less than forty rock'n'roll songs have received this kind of recognition, an honour only achieved when something meets the criterion of being a quintessential part of American culture.

After meeting a Danish girl in the 1980s and moving to Denmark, Link died in Copenhagen in 2005. He was hailed by big names such as Bob

Dylan and Bruce Springsteen. Pete Townshend even said that, without Link Wray, he would never have started playing the guitar.

Other famous foreigners are buried in the crypt, such as the Englishman Peter Appleby, who lived in Denmark in the 18th century and made a thriving business out of delivering rope to the navy out at Holmen. He ended up an extremely rich man and has since had a square named after him in Christianshavn.

THE DECORATIONS OF THE "VED VOLDEN" APARTMENT BUILDING

Ved Volden 1–13, 1425 K
- Access: a programme of guided tours can be found on www.vedvolden.dk
- Admission: free
- Metro: Christianshavn

13 surreal entrances

I n 1939, the Norwegian–American artist Elsa Thoresen (1906–1994) together with her husband, the Danish artist Vilhelm Bjerke Petersen (1909–1957), decorated the entrances of the Christianshavn apartment building called "*Ved Volden*" with a total of 13 paintings, one for each entrance.

The 13 paintings do not represent a coherent story and can be viewed independently from one another. Nonetheless, their mysterious and surreal style and the atmosphere created by the paintings are a unifying factor. The background to them was the idea, current in the 1930s, that art should rid itself of museums: it should be where people were – at work and at home. For that reason, the imagery used should also be of everyday things which were very familiar to people. Some of the designs in the 13 entrances are drawn from contemporary popular culture, but they are mixed in with archetypal images, such as the child preparing to go out into the big wide world, the lonely man, or birds flying across the sky.

Among the cultural references, you see a boy who is flying towards the horizon on the back of a bird, a reference to the novel by Swedish author Selma Lagerlöf, *The Wonderful Adventures of Nils*. The artists also made extensive use of simple optical illusions – a *trompe-l'œil* technique that was popularly used in magazines at the time. Perhaps the best example of this is where the trunk and branches of a moonlit tree form a reclining female figure.

Most of the paintings also contain elements taken from the contemporary international art scene: several of the skyscapes cannot be imagined without reference to the work of the Belgian artist René Magritte, while the work whose main image is of a sailing boat is a clear reference to the American artist Edward Hopper's pictures of boats and coastal landscapes.

The paintings very often also represent natural objects such as leaves and stones. Vilhelm Bjerke Petersen called leaves 'children of the air': small, free-moving creatures. And stones, he said, were the 'eggs of eternity': material, rolling their way through history.

LILLE MØLLE

③

Christianshavns Voldgade 54, 1424 K
• Access by special appointment with the National Museum
• Tel: 41 20 60 66
• Open the evening of *Store Bededag* (Great Day of Prayers) and Culture Night
• Metro: Christianshavn

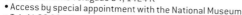

A little mill with great hospitality

To visit Lille Mølle (*Little Mill*) on Christianshavn is to visit an extraordinary home and get a glimpse of a truly unorthodox couple. It is a place that exudes originality, human warmth and great fun.

In the entrance hall, a raincoat hangs alongside a dog's lead – ready for a daily walk on the city ramparts. The big octagonal living room and the library are furnished with Chesterfields where guests were able to relax and be entertained. There is even a little platform where people performed plays, or music perhaps, and, on one wall, there hangs a nude painting of the lady of the house, a gift she gave to her husband in 1945. Everything has been left just as it was in the days when a sociable couple were happy there and lived life to the full.

The couple who turned the mill into their home were Einar Flach-Bundgaard and his wife Johanne. Einar bought the mill in 1916 and they lived there together until his death in 1949. Johanne stayed on until her death in 1974.

Every detail of the decor reflects their ideas and their interests: the dining room, for example, which is decorated in the national romantic peasant style, is a testimony to their thoughts about Schleswig-Holstein. This is a reference to the dispute between Denmark and Prussia over this territory, known to historians as the very complex Schleswig-Holstein Question. In the billiard room there's a drawing of the city of Flensburg, hung with a black mourning ribbon, which was only to be removed on the day when Flensburg became Danish again. Einar and Johanne were dog lovers too and the house has several portraits of their various pets, whose birthdays they apparently always celebrated.

The couple were also passionate collectors of small items of bric-a-brac, or anything else that took their fancy, and the house is testimony to their hobby. Among the miscellany of stuff you will see: Christmas plates, rather garish lamps, books, illegal journals, and liquor bottles and souvenirs collected on their travels around Europe and the United States. But, near their bedroom, there is a special memento: a stray bullet, a wartime souvenir from 22 July 1944, when it came through the bedroom window, whistled over their bed and down the hall where it finally it stopped, wedged in a cupboard door. You can still see it there today.

When they first took over the mill, Einar initiated the idea of preserving it, but it was not until 1973 that, just before her death, Johanne handed it over to the National Museum. The mill was opened to the public in 1996 and since then every effort has been made to maintain its long tradition of hospitality.

HEIBERG'S GARDEN

Behind Søkvæsthuset
Overgaden oven Vandet 58–64, 1415 K
• Metro: Christianshavn

The actress' secret garden

Away from the hustle and bustle of Christiania and the Christianshavn Canal, located right behind the Søkvæsthuset, is a secret garden. Known as Heiberg's Garden, it has a few old trees, some benches and a good view over to the tower of the Church of Our Saviour. To get to it, you go through the courtyard of the Naval Museum and then on through the arched gateway located between the museum and the big yellow annexe, which dates from 1844.

Originally, the garden was created by the actress Johanne Louise Heiberg, who was considered to be the most desirable woman in 19th century Copenhagen. The garden was planted out when she moved into the newly built yellow annexe with her mother-in-law and her husband, the poet and critic Johan Ludvig Heiberg. Since then, it has changed and her famous roses have long since faded and gone, although the oldest trees, which she planted herself, and her staircase are still there. Today, it's easy to appreciate the garden's charm and tranquillity, and, with a little imagination on a dark and windy autumn day, you might 'see' the diva sweeping down the stairs with "a large bonnet on her head, wrapped in something looking like a housecoat", just as one of her neighbours at the time remembered her.

The Heibergs were the most famous couple of the Danish Golden Age. This was a period, usually dating from the early 1800s, when Danish culture revived and flourished again after a series of national calamities which culminated in state bankruptcy in 1813. Like another Greta Garbo, Johanne Louise Heiberg often had to escape from the crowds that swarmed around her when she appeared on the street. Similarly, the great artists and intellectuals of the time flocked around the Heiberg home where Johanne Louise was the centre of attention with her charisma and the beauty of her black hair and blue eyes. Mrs. Heiberg was proud to show off her garden to guests at the house, and a few lucky ones would leave with one of her roses.

But life was far from being blissful: her childhood was marked by poverty and drunkenness and stood in stark contrast to the life she came to live as an adult. In addition, the marriage between these two powerful personalities was very complicated and Johanne Louise often used her garden as a night-time refuge where she would wander among her roses trying to find some peace for her troubled mind.

SCOUT MUSEUM

Arsenalvej 10, 1436 K
• www.spejdermuseet.dk
• Open Thurs 2pm–5pm, Sun 11am–3pm; and (1 May to 30 September)
Wed 5pm–8pm
• Admission: free
• Metro: Christianshavn, Havnebussen

Be prepared!

The now very fashionable Holmen neighbourhood is home to a small Scout Museum that traces the history of the Danish Scout Movement.

Robert Baden-Powell, the founder of the Scout Movement along with his wife, Olave Baden-Powell, achieved near-cult status because of their achievements. In some photos, you see them rubbing shoulders with Danish celebrities such as King Christian X and Crown Princess Ingrid.

From its beginnings in England in 1907, the movement spread like wildfire. Just a few years later, it had branches in Australia, Canada and South Africa and, in 1910, most of the countries of Europe followed, including Denmark.

Baden-Powell was a man with a mission. With a Stetson on his head and sporting a neckerchief, he founded the movement with the aim of educating children to be responsible and independent-minded. There was a military background to this as Baden-Powell's own professional experience came from serving in the British army, but the movement's success was undoubtedly also based on his personal charisma together with the Scout Movement's ability to spice up its serious purpose with some fun.

The museum owns a remarkable collection of sculptures inspired by both Native American and African tribes. One of the finest figures is *Djackomba*, which, according to one of the information labels, was carved in great secrecy in an apartment on Amager. Djackomba's hair is made of dozens of iron nails, which, over time, some specially chosen people were allowed to hammer into his head. In 1935 both King Christian X and his wife, Queen Alexandrine, took part in the fun.

The Scout Museum is run by volunteers, all of whom have a long history in the movement; their personal experiences are one of the great assets of the place. However, if scouting is somewhat unfamiliar to you, "Be prepared" – using the Scouts' own motto – for you might be in for a surprise.

BOATHOUSES AT HALVTOLV

6

Halvtolv, 1436 Copenhagen K
• Metro: Christianshavn, Bus 9A: Havnebussen

A special atmosphere

If you're looking for an enjoyable stroll, a nice view and a little bit of Danish history, you should make your way down to the end of Arsenalvej. Turn left at the yellow buildings, squeeze through a hole in the hedge, make your way along the little gravel path and you'll soon find yourself at the water's edge. From there you'll have a view of the striking houses belonging to the Christiania Commune and, at the end of the road, in Halvtolv, you'll see two impressive black wooden buildings, right on the edge of the water.

Today, these two old military boathouses have been put to new use: one is occupied by the Halvtolv Boat Club (at the beginning of the season, it is packed with boats that have been berthed there for the winter). The boathouse next door is called the Cannon House (*Kanonskuret*) and is used as a community centre by the neighbourhood housing cooperative.

From here, you'll have a beautiful view over the water and, if you're lucky, a glimpse of a bather jumping into the cold water from the old quay in front of the boathouses – something which happens even in winter as it's the haunt of brave souls who swim all year round!

The boat club is private and only for the use of members of the housing cooperative, but you are always welcome to have a seat and soak up its special atmosphere.

The two boathouses were built in the mid-1800s to store the navy's special gunboats, which were first powered by oars and later by steam. The two boathouses that you can see in Halvtov today are the last survivors on this location. Originally, there were many more.

The area is called Halvtolv (Half Twelve) because the boathouses were in a military area called Section 12, and also because the last shed in the group was only half the length of the others.

MASTING CRANE

Nyholm
A. H. Vedels Plads 22, 1439 K
• Access on Culture Night or on one of the special guided tours arranged by the Royal Danish Naval Museum (see www.orlogsmuseet.dk)
• Bus 9A: Havnebussen

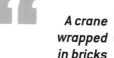

A crane wrapped in bricks

The Masting Crane is one of the most remarkable buildings in Copenhagen harbour. Surprisingly, its masonry has no structural role at all: it is merely a screen which protects the timber interior (the crane itself is inside). It is constructed from a multitude of huge interlocking beams which jointly lift the crane up floor by floor.

While there, be sure to take a trip up to the roof where you'll find one of the best panoramic views of Copenhagen.

The Masting Crane was built for the navy, which required a real heavyweight of a machine. When completed in 1750, it was a modern technical wonder, designed to raise the lower masts, the heaviest ones on a sailing ship. However,

the crane alone was not enough: raw muscle power was needed too. Three capstans were installed on either side of the building. These were turned by teams of sailors and from there the ropes passed into the building through two open doors, one on each side. They were then raised floor by floor until they finally reached the head of the crane. Raising and lowering a lower mast required great skill. When balancing pieces of timber that could weigh as much as 20 tons, any uncontrolled movement could have had disastrous consequences – here, the Masting Crane came into its own.

The architect of the Masting Crane, Philip de Lange (1704–66), was a Dutchman who came to Copenhagen at the age of 24. He designed many other buildings in Holmen. He was also responsible for the Asiatic Company's building in Christianshavn and the two-storey buildings in the yellow town of Nyboder.

THE NAVAL MUSEUM'S MODEL MAKER'S GUILD

8

The navy's former jailhouse at Nyholm
A. H. Vedel Plads 6, 1439 K
• www.modelbyggerlaug.dk
• Access on Culture Night
• Bus 9A: Havnebussen

Based in the navy's former prison at Nyholm, the Model Makers' Guild attracts volunteers and model-making enthusiasts who build superb model ships.

The best models in town

The place also boasts a private library and its own collection of blueprints. And if the model makers cannot find the material they require in the library, they can consult the National Archives in their ongoing search for original drawings, construction contracts and carpentry specifications … because everything must be both historically accurate and to the correct scale. This means it may take years to finish a single model, using selected Bavarian lime wood, the model maker's own rope work and a special sewing machine for the sails.

Previously, model ships were mostly produced for the practical use of naval architects and constructors. Today, however, the model makers work to disseminate the technical and military achievements of the Royal Danish Navy from its foundation in 1510 right up to the present day.

The guild also constructs models of significant buildings with naval connections: in recent years, one major project has been to produce a model of Philip de Lange's Masting Crane (see page 91). Once finished, the model – which is fully functional – will be placed inside the Masting Crane to show students how it actually worked.

At Christianshavn, the Royal Danish Naval Museum boasts one of the world's finest collections of model ships. Part of the credit goes to the Model Makers' Guild, as it is the museum's principal supplier of models.

MADEIRA VINES

Nyholm
• Access: the vines can be seen on several of Nyholm's east- and south-facing walls
• Metro: Christianshavn, Havnebussen

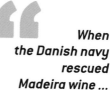

When the Danish navy rescued Madeira wine ...

Visit Nyholm in late summer and you will see lots of grape vines growing on its east- and south-facing walls. Strangely, the vines are the physical evidence of one of the Danish navy's major rescue operations.

Until 1917, when Denmark sold its three islands in the West Indies – St Thomas, St John and St Croix, known today as the U.S. Virgin Islands – the navy had two ships that took turns being stationed there. The ship that had been relieved of its duties made its way home via the island of Madeira off the west coast of Africa. Here it took on fresh supplies. Around 1870, one of the ships, in addition to the normal supplies of fresh fruit and water, also took on board a few Madeira vines. This would prove to be extremely fortunate as, only a few years later, in 1873, the island's vines were attacked by the malignant phylloxera virus: none of them survived.

When a Danish diplomat, who had served in the navy, learned of the disaster, he immediately suggested replanting Madeira's vineyards with cuttings from the vines growing in Copenhagen. These were found thriving on a south-facing wall in Nyboder and the cuttings were quickly sent back to their country of origin, where their introduction saved the production of sweet Madeira wine.

Today, the vines can be seen in many places with naval connections. Grapes can be found not only in Nyholm, but also in the Kuglegården on Arsenaløen, home to the Defence Command, where a few bottles of Madeira are produced every year. Unfortunately, as it is a Defence establishment, it is difficult to visit.

The Dutch and British navies also claim to have helped save the production of Portuguese Madeira wine in the 1870s.

SKABELONLOFTET

Refshaleøen
Refshalevej 171 A, 1432 K
• Open when there is somebody in the workshops
• Best to visit in the summer
• Bus 40: Havnebussen

Workshop with a view

Far out on Refshaleøen, one of the old industrial B&W (Burmeister & Wain) buildings has been converted into a community workshop whose high ceilings overlook the waters of the Øresund.

Although this former shipbuilding plant appears private, it is accessible by means of a long, steep staircase that runs along the façade with its great expanse of industrial windows, several of which are broken.

At the top of the staircase, the white sign which reads "*Skabelonloftet*" (literally meaning "loft of models") is a reminder of the days when B&W, a ship-designing company, used the ceiling to display full-scale models of ships under construction.

When B&W closed in 1996, the buildings were left empty. Today, Skabelonloftet consists of seventeen workshops, which are rented out to architects, designers and artists. Several of the workshops face onto a long corridor which is panelled with large windows, so, when you walk along it, you

can catch a glimpse of what is going on in the cosy interiors. It is rather like an enclosed miniature city where the corridor acts as the city's main street and the workshops, on either side, function as little homes equipped with stairs, doors and windows of their own. At the end of the corridor, the common-room windows offer a magnificent view of the Øresund. It is best to visit Skabelonloftet in the summer as the place is very cold in winter and many of the tenants are therefore not present.

EXECUTION SHED AT CHRISTIANIA

2nd Redan at Norddyssen behind Christiania
• Access: the execution shed is located behind the third house on the left after the Dysse Bridge
• Metro: Christianshavn

The gloomy remains of the war

If you cross the Dysse Bridge in Christiania heading in the direction of Norddyssen and turn left, you will see some distinctive arrow-shaped buildings. They look like triangular farmhouses and have open courtyards which face on to the moat. Today the houses are cosy dwellings for Christianites, but most of them were originally erected as ammunition depots from 1779 to 1791 as part of Copenhagen's old system of fortifications.

Behind the third house (counting from the bridge) lies an almost invisible, but very gruesome piece of Danish history. Here, near the path, half-hidden in the grass, are some concrete foundations with a little drain: they are the last remnant of an execution shed where thirty people were shot dead between 1946 and 1950.

The many legal cases brought against collaborators and criminals in the wake of the Second World War led Denmark to reintroduce the death penalty for a few years. This meant that execution sheds were built in Viborg and on the Dyssen in Copenhagen. Here, people who had been convicted of killing members of the Resistance, assisting the Gestapo or carrying out acts of counter-sabotage were shot.

As all the executions took place at night, the shed was illuminated by temporary mounted spotlights. The shed consisted of a rear wall made of loose wooden boards that could easily be replaced when the bullets had ripped through them. In addition to the policemen who carried out this gruesome task, a doctor and a priest were always present. A truck carrying coffins waited in the courtyard of a nearby building from where the bodies were taken directly for cremation and buried in the cemetery the following morning.

The last man to be executed in the shed was a 40-year-old Gestapo member, Ib Birkedal Hansen. His execution took place at 1.00 am on 20th July 1950. Soon afterwards the shed was torn down, leaving behind only the concrete foundations with the drain where much blood had been spilled.

THE ABANDONED *PRØVESTENEN* ALLOTMENT ASSOCIATION

Access is obtained from the east side of Kløvermarken via the paths in the area between Raffinaderivej 10 and 20 leading in the direction of *Prøvestenen*

• Metro: Lergravsparken, Bus 77, 40

The quiet, abandoned gardens

I f you follow the perimeter of the Kløvermarken along Raffinaderivej you'll come to a dirt road leading down to the water. Climb through a hole in the fence: from there you'll have a spectacular view of the industrial buildings on the neighbouring islet of *Prøvestenen*, and the surreal prospect of a rusty, deserted quay. It's not just an urban wasteland, however, but is also rather a paradise for wildlife and you may see several species of birds, salamanders and even the rare green toad.

Continue along the path to the left with the quay on your right and you'll come to big piles of rubble. If you're there in summer you can expect to see graceful red poppies swaying on top of them too. Now look around to see if you can make out the almost indiscernible paths that once marked the land used by *Prøvestenen,* the allotment association.

In September 2010, big trucks took away the little huts and the residents said goodbye to their little oasis, which, for sixty years, had been the site of one of the most beautifully situated allotment associations in Copenhagen. Most of them moved to a new address on Lossepladsvej, on Amager Common.

Today, only the most persistent of flowers and memories are left. You can still wander amongst poppies of all colours, purple butterfly bushes, Japanese anemones, bindweed and red roses, and see the little bits and pieces of the place's former life scattered around you, in the form of a little white picket fence, a red and a blue clog hammered onto a pole, and, in the middle of it

all, a sad little bent flagpole. It is quiet here, and the once well-tended, but now overgrown gardens, and an occasional broken flowerpot have all transformed it into a secluded wilderness. The place exudes an air both of sad desolation and the peace of undisturbed nature.

During World War II, the area had two metres of industrial waste dumped on it. For this reason the soil is severely contaminated by residues of oil, heavy metals and tar, and in recent years, the residents of the allotments were not allowed to grow vegetables.

PAINTINGS BY HANS SCHERFIG

Kofoeds Skole, Nyrnberggade 1, 2300 S
• Open Mon–Thurs 8am–4pm, Fri 8am–2pm
• Metro: Lergravsparken

Dreams of Africa

From the outside, *Kofoeds Skole* (school), on the island of Amager, resembles many other buildings of the 1970s. Yet inside everything is very different, with a large painting covering the entire back wall of the lobby. This is a jungle scene by the artist and writer Hans Scherfig (1905–79), painted in 1959: here, enormous easy-going elephants with strange trunks flap their ears; there, a herd of antelope scamper across the plains. From the treetops, large curious eyes, perhaps a group of lemurs, try to intimidate you – at the same time, they keep you away from the riverbanks where crocodiles are lurking, smirking. Even the frame comes alive as a little hedgehog runs around it.

It is also interesting to see Scherfig's other work, *Sun on the Savannah*, painted in 1977 and displayed in the school conference room on the fourth floor. Although the room is regularly occupied, the staff will be happy to show you around. Here Scherfig is in his element, with an African painting in tones of yellow, populated by two solitary rhinoceros looking tenderly at one another across the savannah.

Scherfig, an avowed communist and socially engaged writer, always considered painting as a game, which he only did for the pleasure it gave him – perhaps this explains why most recognised critics have had great difficulty in understanding his work. Although Scherfig never went to Africa himself, the continent's animals were a source of inspiration throughout his life. It stuck in his mind as a fantastic place onto which he could project his dreams of a better world. A world without conflict, made up of caring animals – and plants – living in harmony where nothing good or evil happens.

Somehow, since it was founded in 1928, *Kofoeds Skole* – which has always defended the most vulnerable members of society – seems the ideal place for his paintings.

HEROLD'S VAREHUS

Øresundsvej 21A, 2300 S
• www.heroldsvarehus.dk
• Open Tues 10.30am–5pm, Wed–Fri 10.30am–5.30pm, Sat 10am–2pm
• Metro: Lergravsparken

*Copenhagen
in the 1920s*

Located in one of the area's few remaining buildings from the mid-1800s, Herold's Varehus is a piece of living cultural history. It is particularly well known for its sale of joke and novelty items: its tightly packed shelves offer boxes of stink bombs and fart pillows, as well as toy guns.

Nowhere else does Copenhagen have anything remotely resembling Herold's. Here you step into a piece of untouched Copenhagen history, as if nothing had changed since the 1920s.

It is important to take your time since half the pleasure is in listening to the store manager, Connie Hansen, telling you all about the place. The other half is hunting for all the things that you never knew you needed but will take home anyway. If you are missing American flints for your gas-powered pocket lighter, Herold's is the place. If your bike looks a little sad, you can get a flag to stick on your handlebars. Need to secure your hat in a high wind? Snap up an antique hat holder. And if summer insects are driving you crazy, you can buy fly paper … made in 1945. Finally, if you really want to splash the cash, the most expensive item is a handmade miniature horse carriage from 1914 with a price tag of 25,000 DKK.

With the city's rapid growth in the late 19th century, and the equally rapid growth of the working classes, the need arose for cheap entertainment. Henry and Mary Herold saw an opportunity and started the company in 1896 – initially as a hardware store located in Vesterbro. But by 1923, the business had grown to such an extent that larger premises had to be found. The outcome was a move to Øresundsvej to the current building, which measures only 100 m².

Henry and his son Stanley invented and produced a wide selection of toys and cheap jewellery. To continue expanding the business, Stanley went to Germany in 1930 to buy up an entire warehouse full of goods. They continued this business strategy throughout the 1940s and 1950s, but, around 1960, the store began to focus more on retail than, as previously, on wholesale deals with amusement parks and travelling circuses. Today, it is the fourth generation of Henry and Mary's descendants who stand behind the counter.

THE FRESCOES
OF SAINT ELISABETH OF THURINGIA

15

Forebyggelsescenter Amager
Hans Bogbinders Allé 3, 2300 S
• Open during normal office hours
• Metro: Amagerbro

*Eight years
with Elisabeth*

Formerly known as the Saint Elisabeth Hospital, the branch of the Amager Hospital at Hans Bogbinders Allé has an extraordinary, but little known fresco. Three hundred and fifty square metres in size, it extends up four flights of stairs. It was painted by Jais Nielsen and depicts the life of Saint Elisabeth of Thuringia (1207–1231).

Elizabeth had an eventful, if short life. Born a princess of Hungary she was removed from her family as a child and taken abroad where she became engaged to the son of the Landgrave of Thuringia. He met an early death, however, and so, when she was thirteen, Elisabeth was married to another son of the same house. At eighteen she was already the mother of three children but found herself a widow again at nineteen. She then met her own death at the age of twenty four.

One of the most famous legends associated with Elisabeth is that of the 'Miracle of the Roses', which is depicted on the wall at the entrance. Elisabeth was known for her compassion, and, during a famine, she handed out bread to the poor. This kind act had, unfortunately, met with her husband's disapproval and so she had to smuggle the bread out of the castle's storerooms, tucked away in the folds of her long dress. On her way out, she bumped into her husband and told him that she was only carrying roses. On being forced to prove this, the miracle happened: the bread had turned into roses.

It took Jais Nielsen eight years to paint the life of Elisabeth, before

he finally finished it in 1935. The fresco technique involves painting onto fresh lime plaster and this requires the artist to work within an area that can be completed before the wet plaster dries. It requires a great degree of skill and speed to accomplish successfully and it also leaves clear traces of the artist at work. You can still see the outlines of the stencils, which were used to transfer the sketch onto the wall. These appear as fine black dotted lines.

LABOUR INSTITUTION SUNDHOLM

Sundholmsvej 8-59, 2300 S
• Metro: Islands Brygge, Amagerbro

A shelter for dropouts

A room on the second floor of the former weavers' workshop at Sundholm was formerly used as a meeting place and church. This explains why the building has a bell tower as well as an altar with the figure of Christ behind the large double doors at the back.

The Labour Institution Sundholm, its former official name, was built in 1905–08 to replace *Ladegården*, Copenhagen's previous shelter. It was something of a culture shock for those transferred to the new facility, because it adopted a new philosophy to that of the past. It was designed as a working community for the city's dropouts, a place where they could learn a trade and produce some of their own food. To meet a pressing social need, the institution was organised to accommodate more than 1,000 people and had its own gardens, a pigsty, a spacious kitchen and even a morgue ... It also boasted a laundry, carpentry workshop and cobbler, although its greatest pride and joy was the vast weavers' workshop.

Sundholm was an enclave, its perimeter surrounded with barbed-wire fences and, rather more fetchingly, roses and hawthorn hedges. It was also surrounded by a 5-m-deep ditch, which gave "Sundholm" its name: *sund* is Danish for healthy and *holm* means island. In this way the city's outcasts were sequestered in a small space especially for them. Today Sundholm is still a shelter for dropouts, basically homeless people and drug addicts. Here they can find a bed to sleep in, warm clothing and a meal. And it still has a carpentry workshop and laundry. For many, Sundholm is a refuge from the hard life of the streets, a place where you aren't seen as an outsider or subjected to social disapproval – something for visitors to bear in mind.

Although the old church is not open to the public, a walk around the enclave is an experience in itself. Although the ditch has long since been filled in, many of the institution's old buildings have new uses. Crossing the threshold of one of the gates of Sundholm certainly opens your eyes to one of the city's most unusual sites.

BALLOON HANGAR

Artillerivej 73, 2300 S
• Metro: Islands Brygge

From balloon hangar to indoor riding arena

Hidden away behind some tall trees and shrubs on Artillerivej, a small riding school with around twenty-five horses has a very special atmosphere.

The riding school, which opened here in 1961, is installed in a former hot-air balloon hangar dating from 1917. In summer, swallows nest under the roof and swoop about high above the heads of the young riders and their watching parents.

With its oblong wooden structure and curved roof, the hangar is also an impressive remnant of Copenhagen's military history. From 1872, the area was named the Balloon Park and served as a training ground for military personnel, who used the large hot-air balloons to test the range of the cannon balls fired from them over Amager Common. The special elongated shape of this type of balloon – the so-called "dragon" – had been developed because, under windy conditions, it proved more stable than the normal round balloon. When not in use, the balloons were stored in the hangar. Today, its elongated shape makes an ideal small indoor riding arena.

The military personnel who worked in the Balloon Park also lived there, and their red wooden houses today provide a cosy alternative neighbourhood located next to the riding school.

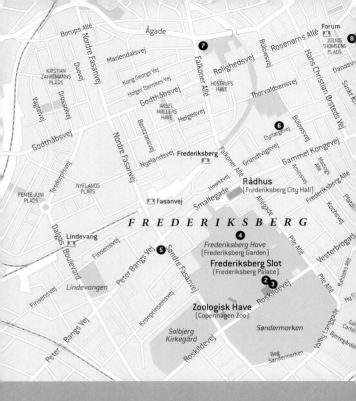

WEST

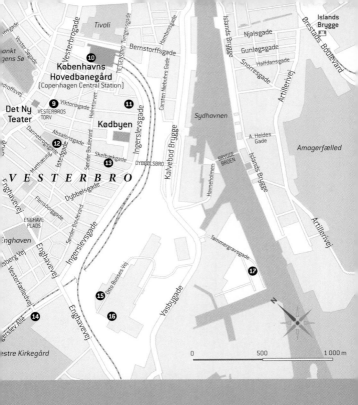

UNCLE TOM'S CABIN

Bjerregårdsvej 16, 2500 Valby
• S-train: Enghave, Valby

The wandering cabin

At the end of a residential street called Bjerregårdsvej stands a curious house built of timber which is just over 3 m wide and whose roof is adorned with exotic dragons' heads. Above the door, a sign reads *"Onkel Toms Hytte"* (Uncle Tom's Cabin).

Until 2005, the house was behind Østerport Station on Folke Bernadottes Allé, where it was first built in 1905. In 2005 the area behind Østerport was undergoing redevelopment and Uncle Tom's Cabin was due for demolition. At the very last minute, however, the house was bought by a private investor who moved it to Bjerregårdsvej.

The cabin was originally a small shop selling goods to the workers in Frihavnen, the nearby harbour area, but it was later enlarged because it was doing such good business. Later, a tobacconist called Jondahl took it over and ran his business from the ground floor while he and his family lived on the first floor. They stayed there until the 1970s and, in its last years on the site, the house was home to a clothes shop selling glamorous women's clothing from the narrow little ground-floor premises.

According to some sources, the house originally stood in Tivoli, where it was part of a major exhibition. When the exhibition closed, the house was dismantled and rebuilt behind Østerport. It apparently got its name because of two children from the Danish West Indies who were put on display there as part of the exhibition. In 1905, the year of the construction of Uncle Tom's Cabin, Tivoli actually did host a colonial exhibition in which 7-year-old Victor and 4-year-old Alberta, from St Croix in the West Indies, were "exhibited" in the middle of the West Indian Pavilion. The children were placed on a table with a white tablecloth and, as if that were not bad enough, at one point, shockingly, they were even moved to a cage because they (especially Victor) kept on escaping to the Greenland section, which they found more exciting.

FROM COPENHAGEN TO WASHINGTON, D.C.

The story of Uncle Tom's Cabin in Copenhagen is strangely linked to the original Uncle Tom's Cabin that inspired Harriet Beecher Stowe's famous 1852 novel.

In 2005, the original Uncle Tom's Cabin, which features in the book, was (just like its Copenhagen counterpart) in danger of being demolished. In a last-minute rescue, the U.S. authorities decided to protect the building, which now stands in its original location in Washington, D.C.

THE MARBLE BATHTUB

Frederiksberg Palace
Roskildevej 28A, 2000 Frederiksberg
• Tours of the palace on the last Saturday of each month – 11am and
1pm – except for July and December. In addition, the bathtub can be
seen all year round by looking through the windows of the basement in
the east wing of the palace (the one facing the Frederiksberg Garden).
• Bus 6A

*Bathed
in sin*

In the basement of the east wing of the Frederiksberg Palace there is something worth a visit. Hidden behind a concealed door, a narrow staircase leads down into the basement where a sunken marble bathtub has been built in the floor. A huge mirror hangs above it, suspended from the ceiling by chains, its now missing original red curtains used to screen the occupant of the bath.

This beautiful marble bathtub was designed by the architect C. F. Harsdorff in 1770. At that time, King Christian VII's personal physician, Johann Friedrich Struensee, seized power in Denmark, but also began an affair with Queen Caroline Mathilde.

Struensee initiated some work on the palace and, according to tradition, built the bathtub for Christian VII, believing that daily baths would have a healing effect on the insane king. The king, however, suffered from claustrophobia and he never got to use it as he had a panic attack the first time he was taken down the narrow staircase.

Instead, it was left to the queen and to Struensee, who, according to legend, used it extensively.

The Frederiksberg Palace was built between 1701–1709 for King Frederik IV and for 150 years it was used as the summer residence of the Danish Royal Family. In 1859 The Royal Danish Army Officers Academy moved into the palace.

POTERNEN

Frederiksberg Palace, Roskildevej 28A, 2000 Frederiksberg
• Access by contacting the Royal Danish Army Officers Academy
(tel: 36 16 26 32). You can also ask to see the *Poternen* on one of the
public tours of the palace
• Bus 6A

The king's secret back door

Built into a hill under Frederiksberg Garden, the *Poternen* is a beautiful vaulted underground passage that can only be visited by special arrangement. The passage connects the palace with the Servants' Yard, which originally consisted of a barn, an indoor riding arena, stables, a smithy and a building for horse-drawn carriages, as well as a kitchen. The needs of the royal household were many and all these areas were required to accommodate the royal family when they went to the palace along with their servants, horses and countless pieces of luggage. In 2012, when the *Poternen* was being restored, vestiges of the palace's past life came to light when oyster shells and fragments of fine glass and porcelain were discovered. The *Poternen* was also the route by which the palace servants could move about, out of sight of their royal masters. It also served as a short cut so that the household servants, stablemen and kitchen staff could get to the palace quickly without having to go all the way around and up the steep hill. At the same time, the *Poternen* served as the king's secret "back door" in case he wanted to leave the palace unnoticed.

Today the *Poternen* still connects the palace to the Servants' Yard but, since 1859, when the Royal Danish Army Officers Academy moved into the palace, the buildings have taken on new functions. Nowadays, parts of the beautiful royal stables have been converted into a gymnasium, the indoor riding arena houses conference rooms and the old smithy is used as a small workshop. Although the Frederiksberg Palace was not built as a fortress, but as a summer palace for King Frederik IV, the name *Poternen* originally referred to a covered back door or a tunnel in a fortress.

NEARBY

THE KING'S STEPPING STONE

Near the entrance to the *Poternen*, the yellow stone with two steps cut into it leaning against the wall was used by King Frederik VI to mount his horse. Similar stepping stones are to be found in the palace grounds beside the old barn down by the Servants' Yard. There is also one in the Royal Stables at the Christiansborg Palace.

THE CENTRE OF FREDERIKSBERG GARDEN ❹

Frederiksberg Garden
Frederiksberg Runddel 1A, 2000 Frederiksberg
• Open all year from sunrise to sunset
• Metro: Frederiksberg

Beyond the paths, where gardens meet

Frederiksberg Garden is a "Romantic-style" garden, which was conceived and laid out in the early 19th century during the reign of King Frederik VI. Start your visit by following the paths which meander between shady trees, where you'll encounter groups of well-fed geese, then continue across the picturesque little bridges. These paths were, in fact, designed to lead visitors on through a fantasy landscape scattered with visual "surprises": a Chinese pagoda, a Greek temple, an artificial barrow and – the epitome of Romantic garden design – a mysterious grotto.

It is a garden to get wonderfully lost in. That is its purpose. There are no straight paths to guide you. Nothing is symmetrical here. There is no centre – or, at least, that is what you are led to believe, for there is a special spot in the garden with another agenda. But to find it, you have to move beyond the paths.

Looking at a map, you will discover that the garden hides a centre, which can only be reached by walking over the lawn next to the Chinese Pavilion. Here, all of a sudden you will find yourself exactly where the former Baroque garden had its centre and where today its two main axes are miraculously preserved. Here, at the very heart of the garden, the existing Romantic garden opens up in the strangest of ways, offering an amazing spatial experience and a look back in time. There are no blocked views, no visual obstacles, no "surprises" – on the contrary, everything is unobstructed in all four directions. It is as if the garden lies at your feet: it all makes sense.

If you'd visited the garden in the 18th century, you would have seen it in its Baroque heyday. It was then designed around two main symmetrical axes. At this point where the two axes met - the centre of the garden where you are now standing - there was an octagonal pavilion where the royal family liked to enjoy a cup of tea after a stroll in the garden. They would have looked out on a garden which was perfectly ordered and controlled in its design. Absolutely straight avenues of lime trees created a framework for the sixty-four symmetrical beds. Perhaps the royal family would also have admired the fine topiary work that had shaped the yew trees and juniper bushes into beautifully precise spherical and cone shapes. With this emphasis on order and geometric precision, this was a very different garden from the one we see today.

ALTAR-BREAD BAKERY AT THE DEACONESS ⑤
DIAKONISSESTIFTELSEN

Peter Bangs Vej 1, 2000 Frederiksberg
- Access upon prior arrangement with *Søsterhjemmet* (tel: 38 38 41 00)
- Metro: Frederiksberg

Three million communion wafers a year

Most people probably don't know that the wafers used in churches during the communion service are usually made in special bakeries. The one that bakes most of the altar bread for the Danish National Church is located at the Deaconess (*Diakonissestiftelsen*) in Frederiksberg and makes an interesting visit. At the same time, you can do a guided tour of the Deaconess, which will introduce you to its work and the fine architecture of its buildings, including the Deaconess' own church, the neo-Gothic Emmaus Church designed by architect, Hans J. Holm.

The Deaconess is next door to a bicycle park and to get to the bakery you need to go down to the low-ceilinged basement. Here, there is a marked

contrast between the bakery's simple setting and the ceremonial of the churches where the sacramental bread is offered. There are no dusty clouds of flour and no smell of freshly baked bread; nor are there any "high priests" to oversee production. The atmosphere is quiet and almost aesthetic, and the clinical production system resembles that of the pharmaceutical industry. The workforce is small and conscientious and the wall decorations consist merely of a certificate from the Danish Veterinary and Food Administration inspectors.

The only thing this bakery has in common with the city's other bakeries is that the day starts with the mixing of the dough – in this case, a very simple one. It consists of nothing more than wheat flour, a little rice flour and some water. The dough, or rather the batter, is poured into a fully automated machine, which then squirts out the shapeless lumps onto a plate by means of plastic tubes. A big metal stamp then impresses a razor-sharp image of Christ on the Cross onto the lumps of dough. Before the finished wafers are ready for their journey to parishes all over the country, they go through a manual quality control and are finally packed in cardboard tubes.

The production of altar bread at Frederiksberg dates back to 1876. At first, the bakery only made bread for its own consumption, but soon other churches became interested and so production expanded. Today, they produce a total of three million wafers a year.

MUSEUM OF VETERINARY MEDICINE

Søndre Sti 4 (Bülowsvej side entrance), 1870 Frederiksberg C
• Visits by appointment with the curator of the museum Hans Henrik Smedegaard
• hhs@life.ku.dk
• Metro: Frederiksberg

> *A small and forgotten university museum*

Consigned to an attic on the Frederiksberg Campus of the University of Copenhagen, the Museum of Veterinary Medicine is a small and forgotten museum with a large collection of equine artefacts.

Notable exhibits include horseshoes, veterinary instruments, masks for anaesthetising horses, skulls, deformed hooves, a model of the old school of veterinary medicine, statuettes of horses and an anvil. There is even a remarkable 19th-century veterinary pharmacy, in perfect condition, which was moved here from Fyn (island of Funen) in 1970. It was originally put together by Kirstine Rash-Nielsen, a vet's wife who collected all kinds of medicinal herbs and concocted a number of drugs herself. Her medicine cupboard, also on display, contains jars and vials still filled with powders and ointments to treat all sorts of ailments, from bovine constipation to swine fever.

However, the heart of the collection consists of 8,000 horseshoes of all shapes and sizes. This collection is all the more important because the farrier – who shod the horses – was behind the establishment of the veterinary school, which in turn developed the veterinary profession as an independent discipline. The horseshoes on display come from Europe and Asia, and many of them have been used as teaching aids for students who learned the art of the farrier as part of their basic veterinary training.

In the mid-18th century, Denmark, like the rest of Europe, was seriously affected by rinderpest: medical students were sent to France to learn more about the disease. One of these students was Peter Christian Abildgaard (see page 159), who later founded the first veterinary school in Denmark, at Christianshavn, in 1773. Although he hadn't actually learned much about rinderpest while in France, he remembered how important it was to shoe horses properly. From then on, the farrier's trade was taught before anything else to the first students of the veterinary school.

Hans Henrik Smedegaard, the museum curator, is getting on in years and none of the students seems keen to take over from him, so don't delay if you want to visit this museum – the 8,000 horseshoes and all the other treasures of this fascinating exhibition may soon be put into storage for good.

THE FALCONRY FARM

The backyard of Falkoner Allé 112 and 120, 2000 Frederiksberg
• Metro: Frederiksberg

The last remains of the king's Falconry Farm

Most people are probably not aware that the densely populated street called Falkoner Allé is named after a falconry farm (*Falkonergården*) where, until 1810, the kings of Denmark kept their hunting falcons. Even fewer people know that some remains of this farm have miraculously survived in an anonymous backyard.

Therefore, it's an almost magical experience to walk through a narrow passage between two tall buildings and find a little yellow house, once a wing of the farm that was built by King Christian V in 1664 when he was Crown Prince. Christian was a hunting enthusiast and he had it built for his Master of Falconry and his falcons. The farm was demolished in 1927, but the little yellow house was left untouched. The building may have been a stable for the horses, which the hunting parties rode, or it may have been the 'dormitory' for the beautiful and very precious falcons from Iceland and Greenland.

Falconry became popular in Denmark in the Middle Ages, and by the 17th and 18th centuries it had become one of the most prestigious pastimes for members of the aristocracy. In Denmark, the kings had the advantage in that they held exclusive rights to the most coveted birds, namely the rare white falcons from Greenland and also those from Iceland, which had very distinctive markings. As they were so prized, kings often gave falcons as gifts to other kings.

The king rode out with his hunting party and his dogs, with his hooded falcon perched on a leather gauntlet on his arm. At the start of the hunt, specially trained dogs were sent to sniff out the prey: herons, partridges or cranes, for instance. When the dogs had frightened the prey into seeking refuge in the sky, the king would "throw" his falcon, which would immediately identify the prey and attack it. The trained falcon forced the prey to the ground, to await the arrival of the king who had ridden in hot pursuit. As a reward, the falcon was fed a piece of fresh meat while the king's servants gathered up the spoils.

By 1810 falconry had gone out of fashion in Denmark and the Falconry Farm was closed. Today the little yellow house is all that's left of the grand royal building and it's now a private residence.

N. H. RASMUSSEN'S GYMNASIUM

8

Today Gotvedskolen
Vodroffsvej 51, 1900 Frederiksberg C
• Access by prior arrangement with Gotvedskolen (tel: 35 35 20 19)
• Metro: Forum

"Straighten your back and speak the truth"

Above the entrance to N. H. Rasmussen's 1898 gymnasium, a sign, written in beautiful Jugendstil letters, reads: "Straighten your back and speak the truth." As both a motto and an instruction, the words summarise the main ideas behind the gymnastics movement which spread throughout the Nordic countries in the late 19th century. Likewise, the architect P. V. Jensen-Klint believed that a beautiful and dignified building helped shape the character of the person who lived in it.

Essentially, the beautiful old gymnasium remains intact and is still in use, just as it was more than 100 years ago. All the equipment in the gym is original, and the washing and changing facilities, which are in the basement, still have the benches, hat racks and cupboards that were used a century ago. The building makes the point that functionality and fine craftsmanship never go out of fashion.

Despite being one of the major pioneers of the gymnastics movement, Rasmussen is not well known in Denmark … and much less so than his daughter, Helle Gotved. She grew up in this gymnasium where, from a very young age, she followed the lessons from the balcony, where she was brought up on the philosophy of "a healthy mind in a healthy body".

However, she soon realised that these old, and very strict, ideas had outlived their usefulness. After the Second World War, she developed her own system known as the *Gotvedskolen,* which is now taught to students in her father's old house. This system is much more in tune with the nature of the human body. It has a more holistic approach, based on creating an awareness of the whole body and its functions, encouraging greater pleasure in one's own body and increasing knowledge of psychosomatic connections. Music is an integral part of the gymnastics programme.

EX-ORIENT BAR

Vela

Viktoriagade 2–4, 1655 V

• Visitors are kindly asked to respect the bar's current existence as a lesbian bar and are therefore urged to come early in the evening

• Open Wed 9pm-12 midnight, Thu 9pm-4am, Fri and Sat 9pm-5am

• S-train: Copenhagen Central Station, Vesterport

> **The city's oldest hooker bar?**

I n Viktoriagade, the Vela bar (new name of the historical Orient bar) has an unusual façade that boasts a series of illustrations of seductive oriental women.

Oddly enough, the best description of the place can be found in Tom Kristensen's 1930 novel *Hærværk* (literally *Vandalism* – published in English as *Havoc* in 1968). On one of his usual binges, the novel's protagonist ends up in "a tiny room decorated in a twisted oriental style, where behind the semi-circular bar was a high altar with bottles and some ugly Buddhas that shone lustfully with coloured light bulbs in their eyes". The room itself was inhabited by "priestesses" with "dark, fiery eyes", and also by "soft, troubled girls". In the novel, the bar is called the "Orient" and there seems to be no doubt that the author was inspired by the real Vesterbro of the 1920s.

Known as "the city's oldest hooker bar" by the locals, Viktoriagade 2-4 has even been the object of a study, when, in 2012, two researchers, Rikke Andreassen and Linda Lapina, from Roskilde University, decided to investigate a little further. They came to two main conclusions: first, that the place has been home to a bar since 1902 and that for an unbroken period of more than a hundred years it was known as the Orient Bar; and second, that the bar's physical layout had been largely unchanged since the 1930s. Of the colourful windows on the front, two are probably original, while four are later replacements. The panelling in the room and the silk wallpaper, which features little Chinese women in a landscape dotted with covered bridges, are clearly from the 1930s.

Despite strenuous efforts, the study could not, however, verify the bar's reputation as "the city's oldest hooker bar". There is no evidence that it had any connection with prostitution, and there was certainly no involvement with Asian women. Its reputation could therefore be put down to "poetic licence".

THE MYSTERIOUS FACE

Vestibule of the Vesterbrogade wing
Copenhagen Central Station, Copenhagen V
• Access from Vesterbrogade
• Copenhagen Central Station

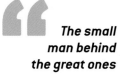

*The small
man behind
the great ones*

I n the vestibule of the Vesterbrogade wing of
Copenhagen Central Station, a mysterious
little face peeks out of the wall situated
between two doors at the entrance. It certainly
wasn't part of the original decoration: the little
figure was, in fact, added in the 1960s by a
long-serving craftsman just before he retired
from his job with the National Railways.

Perhaps it was a little retirement present to himself – a private joke intended
as a teasing counterpoint to the other, rather solemn, stone faces which adorn
the building.

When the Central Station (1908–11) was completed, the Vesterbrogade
vestibule was the main entrance to the building. On the outside, at the
front entrance, you'll see the rather more conventional sculpted heads of
august personalities with railway connections. To the left are the National
Railways' director general, G. C. C. Ambt (with the wings-on-wheel logo of
the National Railways on his cap), and the railway engineer C. F. S. Ernst (with
his huge beard). To the right is the architect of the building, Heinrich Wenck

(with French beret and an elegant
moustache), together with the
director general's son, E. Ambt
(wearing fancy motoring goggles),
who worked as Wenck's assistant.
Inside the impressive 18-m-high
vestibule are two giants of railway
history: on one side, high on a
granite pillar, there's the great
Scottish engineer and developer
of the steam engine, James Watt,
and on the other, one of the great
technical pioneers of locomotives
and the railways, the Englishman
George Stephenson.

SECRET COPENHAGEN 133

THE TOTAL WAR GRAFFITO

⓫

The Meat-Packing District, *Tvillingehallen* (today *Billedskolen*)
Staldgade 35, 1699 V
• S-train: Copenhagen Central Station

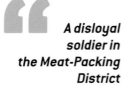

A disloyal soldier in the Meat-Packing District

Today, on what was once a yellow brick wall, you can still see the remains of an old graffito, which is a peculiar, yet touching riposte to one of the most famous speeches of World War II. These clumsily carved letters are on the *Tvillingehallen*, a building which today houses the municipality of Copenhagen's art school (*Billedskolen*). On the side of the building which faces the central station, someone has written these words on a brick which you'll find on the far right-hand side of the wall: "Wollt ihr den totalen Krieg?" (Do you want total war?), followed by the reply: "Nein" (No).

This question was posed by Dr. Joseph Goebbels, the German propaganda minister. The reply, scratched on the wall, is the work of an anonymous German soldier on patrol in the area, but someone with a mind of his own.

On 18 February 1943, Goebbels gave what was probably his most famous speech. It has since gone down in history as the *Sportpalast* speech, named after the indoor sports arena in Berlin where it was delivered. The recent setbacks the troubled German army had sustained served as the impetus for the speech. In January, the Germans had lost to the Allies in North Africa, followed in early February by their defeat at the Battle of Stalingrad. Unless every effort was made to reverse the situation, Germany was facing defeat. Therefore, February 1943 was a crucial time. The first step was to inform the German people how vital their continuing support for the war effort was going to be and to prepare them for even more suffering.

Goebbels' speech has also been called the "totaler Krieg" speech, or "total war" speech after one of the rhetorical questions he yelled at the thousands of spectators gathered in the Berlin Sportpalast: "I ask of you: Do you want total war? And if necessary, do you want a war more devastating and radical than anything we can imagine today?" And the answer came back promptly from the crowd – a massive and hysterical: "YES".

During the Occupation, German soldiers were deployed to patrol areas of strategic importance, including places vital for the security of provisions. With its butchers' halls, the Meat-Packing District in Vesterbro was one such place. Several of the German soldiers who patrolled there have left behind little scratched graffiti, most of which are just names they carved as testimony to the endless, tedious nights they spent patrolling in Copenhagen.

SHOOTING LANE WALL ⑫

Istedgade 72–74, 1650 V
• S-train: Copenhagen Central Station, Dybbølsbro

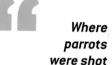

Where parrots were shot

There's another piece of quirky Copenhagen history to be found behind a rather medieval-looking wall which connects numbers 72 and 74 in Istedgade. Behind the wall you'll see a children's playground, with a chute contained in a colourful model of a huge parrot. This bird is actually an indicator of the past function of the wall, which isn't medieval at all, but dates from 1887.

In Danish, the expression 'shooting the parrot' is used to describe somebody who is lucky and the phrase has its origins in the sport that was practised on this site in Vesterbro.

The Royal Shooting Society had its premises on a rather narrow neck of land that ran all the way from Vesterbrogade to where the railway tracks are today; its previous location was beside the shoreline.

The highlight of the year was a shooting competition where a wooden parrot was used as a target. Originally, the bird was placed on a pole out by the shore, but when the railway to Roskilde was opened in 1847, the shooting lane had to be moved further into Vesterbro. The Shooting Lane Wall was erected later on. The parrot, on its pole, provided a target for the marksmen, but it had to be stationed in front of the wall, which was built both to prevent unauthorized people from entering the society's premises and to stop people being hit by stray bullets.

You can still see the bullet holes at the top of the wall. Members of the society who had a better aim and actually 'shot the parrot' were celebrated with the title of 'King of the Bird'.

> Originally, shooting birds was a medieval sport that was used to train knights for battle. It spread from southern Europe to Denmark, where the first shooting societies emerged in the 15th century. Over time, the sport lost its military importance and became more of an enjoyable social occasion, where the shooting was accompanied by a lot of eating and drinking. In Copenhagen, such festivities were celebrated in the Royal Shooting Society's clubhouse, built during the period 1782 to 1787 at the end of the shooting lane facing Vesterbrogade. Today, the house is home to the Museum of Copenhagen.

THE OLGA'S LYST TOY MUSEUM

Sommerstedsgade 11, 1718 V
• Access only upon prior arrangement
• Tel: 33 23 85 58 or 60 89 85 58
• Admission: child 30 DKK, adult 50 DKK
• S-train: Dybbølsbro

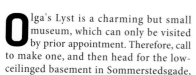

In a world of small things

Olga's Lyst is a charming but small museum, which can only be visited by prior appointment. Therefore, call to make one, and then head for the low-ceilinged basement in Sommerstedsgade, where you'll experience two hundred years of Danish cultural history in this small, but densely packed, space. The exhibits will give you an insight into how, over the years, Danish society has viewed its children's upbringing, and, in particular, the role that was assigned to little girls. The museum's 19th-century dolls' houses, in particular, provide an enlightening glimpse of the latter. To a large extent, they were used as training grounds for the little daughters of the bourgeoisie. The houses were toys which taught good housekeeping methods, so that, once the girls got married, they already knew what was required of them.

Consequently, around 1900, the toy industry, which was producing the houses and all their accoutrements, flourished. It was making miniature versions of real Danish homes which replicated the furniture and fittings in each room exactly, right down to the vases and statuettes in the living room, the enamelled metal and copperware in the kitchen, and wardrobes full of clothing, too. And if the master of the house had international interests, it was also possible to subscribe to either the *Journal de Genève* or the *Wiener Zeitung* – printed, of course, in tiny, tiny letters.

Most of the equipment is of German manufacture, but much of it is also homemade. In fact, it was a favourite pastime for fathers to make doll's house furniture out of the wood from their cigar boxes.

The museum also displays teddy bears and dolls. There are examples of the classic Steiff bear as well as a large range of classic girl dolls with perfect rosy cheeks. There are snow-white, glazed porcelain heads and dark-brown African children and, of course, Barbie is there too, introducing another view of womanhood. In addition, there are character dolls – dolls that resemble real people: an example of this is the German 'Kaiser Baby', a popular doll at the time, allegedly depicting the German Emperor Wilhelm II as a baby.

COPENHAGEN PRISON MUSEUM

14

Vestre Fængsel, Vestre Kirkegårds Allé 1A, 2450 SV
- www.koebenhavnsfaengsler.dk
- Access Tues 10am–4pm
- Admission: 20 DKK
- S-train: Enghave

*Ingenuity
behind bars*

Created in 1994 at Vestre Fængsel jail, the Copenhagen Prison Museum offers a glimpse of the history and the lives played out behind the prison walls since it was built in 1895. Entrance is via a locked gate, and just behind it is the closed area which could house up to 430 inmates.

Over four floors, there is so much history and so many stories on offer that one visit isn't enough to do the museum justice. Walking along the top floor gives you a real feeling of what it was like to be imprisoned there, and you even get the opportunity to look into a couple of the new cells. Up here, the place is packed with artefacts: assorted truncheons, handcuffs, old photos and a very moth-eaten straitjacket.

The exhibition also shows some of the imaginative ways in which prisoners tried to contact the outside world or escape either the tedium of prison life or the place itself. These include: a plea to the kitchen for better food scratched on the soot-encrusted bottom of a china plate; a love letter that was hidden in one of the prisoner's mouths; and snuff smuggled in two hollow eggs. Another case contains a collection of homemade keys and a dictionary with a hole cut out of it to fit a mobile phone. And so it goes on. The remaining floors have escape ladders made from picture frames, and the traditional knotted bed sheets and clothing left over from yet another bid for freedom.

Vestre Fængsel once had a large carpentry workshop where inmates learned woodworking skills, so the museum also boasts a large collection of colourful wooden toys. Among the items on display are horses, doll's house furniture, trams, miniature DSB-ferries and – in the less child-friendly section – a naughty girl on a motorcycle and a miniature model of Hitler lying in his coffin.

The visit ends in the basement, which has an old coffin used to restrain unruly prisoners, as well as a large selection of whips, known as cats-o'-nine-tails. And if you have still not had enough, you can see a reconstruction of the cell which belonged to a woman nicknamed *Englemagersken* (Maker of Angels), who was incarcerated there after receiving a life sentence for killing at least nine infants. Although she was paid to take care of the children, she took the money, killed the children and burned their bodies in her stove.

YELLOW VILLAGE

On the railroad area on Otto Busses Vej
• Access: the most adventurous access to the area is via the tunnel on
Enghavevej, but you can also reach it by Vasbygade
• S-train: Sydhavn, Enghave

An enchanting oasis

A tunnel between Enghavevej and Otto Busses Vej connects Copenhagen to a place which might have come out of a fairy tale. Cycle through the tunnel and you'll end up in a secluded village by the side of some train tracks. This little enchanted world, with its gaily painted yellow houses, is hidden away from the thousands of unsuspecting suburban train passengers who pass by every day.

Not surprisingly, it is known as the Yellow Village and it's an oasis in the middle of the city. Children run around between the cottages where, on warm summer evenings, the residents have barbecues in their little gardens. The Yellow Village is reminiscent of an old village with cottage gardens full of hollyhocks, that, strangely enough, has survived the tidal wave of modern urban redevelopment.

However, the yellow houses are not actually very old because even as late as the beginning of the 20th century, the area was still just part of the seabed. When the nearby Central Station was built, the land was back-filled with soil and old porcelain: this was to create the foundations of dwellings built for the railway workers who moved into these yellow houses and went to work in the huge Central Maintenance Facility right next to them. The point of living so close to the tracks was that the workers could react quickly in emergencies such as train crashes or when there were problems on the line. But today only about half of the inhabitants have a job connected with the railway. The rest are newcomers from the outside world.

OTTO FREDERIK AUGUST BUSSE (1850–1933)

Otte Busse was the son of a machine technician at the Zealand Railway Company (Det Sjællandske Jernbaneselskab). He first trained as a blacksmith, and later as an engineer. He then came to work at the Central Maintenance Facility, which was then situated by Sankt Jørgen Lake, close to the old Central Station.

Busse was a gifted visionary who dedicated his life to trains. In 1892, he became head of the Danish National Railways (DSB) Engine Department, where he was behind the construction of locomotives and snow ploughs as well as coaches. Busse's last major task for the DSB was the moving of the Central Maintenance Facility to the address that today bears his name.

CENTRAL MAINTENANCE FACILITY (*CENTRALVÆRKSTEDET*) ⑯

• Access: the area is often open for Culture Night in September, Open House in October and for other special events

A treat for train enthusiasts

If, instead of going straight to the Yellow Village (see previous page), you turn right after the tunnel between Enghavevej and Otto Busses Vej, you will find yourself in the area known as the Central Maintenance Facility (*Centralværkstedet*) – formerly the heart of operations of the Danish National Railways (DSB). Today the area, with its huge workshops and shunting yards, is being developed for other purposes, but many parts are still untouched, so you can see them in their original state.

If you approach from the back, you will come across a rather romantic overgrown hinterland hidden away behind the village. The first things you'll see are some imposing black full-timbered houses, which, apart from

their colour, make the place look like a deserted old Swedish village whose inhabitants have long ago emigrated to America. Built in 1909 as storage halls for the timber used for the trains, the group of houses is called *Trægården* (the Timber Farm). Grass now grows high between the houses, but the smell of timber testifies to the fact that the buildings are still alive and healthy although several of the roofs have huge holes in them. There are gardens full of apple trees, and in one corner an entire bed is "planted" with hundreds of old bicycles that were probably found abandoned close to railway tracks around Copenhagen.

And just when you think it doesn't get much better, you find yourself in the middle of a cemetery for old trains. Remnants of the last hundred years of railway heritage lie tangled in bindweed while the sun shines in through the cracks. The wagons and locomotives look like something from the Wild West – from the days when trains had little verandas with railings round them at the back of the coaches and tiny delicate panes of glass in their ceilings.

Now staff from the Danish Railway Museum have moved into a nearby building to begin restoring some of the coaches; however, several are in a desperate state and may be beyond repair. So if you want to experience this unique place, hurry up and get on your bike – the area is being redeveloped fast and no one knows what the final outcome will be.

THE SYDHAVNEN 'HALL OF FAME'

Between Landvindingsvej and Enghave Brygge
Sydhavnen
• S-train: Dybbølsbro

A playground for graffiti artists

Graffiti artists in Copenhagen don't need to tag and run. They can take their time and produce works of art. Their 'playground' is a big open courtyard behind the huge red building of the H. C. Ørsted Power Station, where their 'Hall of Fame' can be found: a fantastic place where a whole generation of graffiti artists have been able to go and practise their skills, in broad daylight and without having to look over their shoulders.

Most of the works of art won't last very long. Like the ones on the S-trains they soon disappear beneath new ones sprayed on by another artist. There is one exception, however. This is the *Evolution* graffiti that was created during the summers of 1999 and 2000 by the graffiti artist Ulrik Schiødt, supported by finance from the neighbouring power station. Indeed, no one has ever dared to touch this monumental 170-metre long mural that depicts the beginning of evolution from the Big Bang onwards and features mammoths, dinosaurs and ferocious giant squids. Now and then the question arises of whether the *Evolution* mural needs to be protected. This will surely need to be addressed one day because any development of the waterfront will be the end of the 'Hall of Fame'.

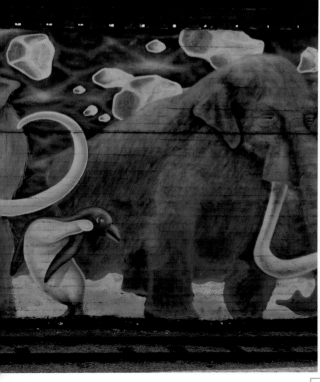

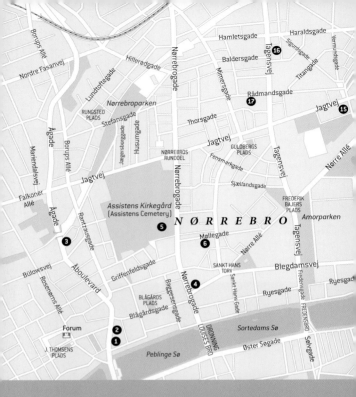

NORTH

BETHLEHEM CHURCH

Åboulevard 8, 2200 N
• Open every Sunday for Mass at 10am
• Metro: Forum

Grundtvig's Church in miniature

Although churches everywhere are designed as pathways from here to the hereafter, between this world and the next, this idea is given a particularly potent meaning in Bethlehem Church (*Bethlehemskirken*) on Åboulevard.

The church, wedged between several other buildings in Copenhagen's busiest street, is separated from the bustle of the city by a single red-brick wall: there is no main porch and entry is directly from the street through small side doors. The traffic might rumble by outside the building but everything is quiet and peaceful inside, an oasis sheltered from the noise and pollution.

Bethlehem Church was built between 1935 and 1937 by one of the major figures of modern Danish history, the architect Kaare Klint (1888–1954). It is a smaller version of the masterpiece designed by his father, Peder Vilhelm Jensen-Klint – Grundtvig's Church at Bispebjerg Bakke.

The best way to describe the Church of Bethlehem is probably to compare the two buildings. Although they both share the same Gothic architecture, Bethlehem, unlike Grundtvig's, is not designed as a separate entity from the city, it literally melts into it.

The central nave of Kaare Klint's church is not as long as his father's, so that it is perceived to be wider and higher. Nor does Bethlehem Church feature the impressive façade of the great Grundtvig's Church. However, these differences in no way affect its special atmosphere. The interior of the building is particularly interesting because it gives the impression of being in a cave dug out of the mountainside: the walls, pillars and arches have indeed been built from plain yellow brick to a height of 18 m, thus creating a harmonious cocooning sensation that immediately brings a feeling of peace.

STONE OF DESTINY

Åboulevard 16, 2200 N
• Metro: Forum

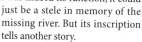

In memory of a tragic drowning

As is the case with many of Copenhagen's religious buildings, Bethlehem Church has no graveyard. Yet beside Åboulevard 16 is a strange stone that could indeed be taken for a funerary monument.

The slim pyramid rising from the pavement bears the date 26–27 November 1812. The stone used to stand in the middle of the River Ladegård, which was covered over in the 1890s to ease the traffic flow around the city and now runs unnoticed below Åboulevard.

Some people believe that the stone was used as a water-level indicator before the river disappeared underground. If that was indeed its function, it could

just be a stele in memory of the missing river. But its inscription tells another story.

During the night of 26–27 November 1812, two women were returning home from a party in the Frederiksberg district. The carriage in which they were travelling left the road and fell into the river. Although history does not record the coachman's fate, the two women were drowned.

We don't know when the inscription was made, but it might date from the time when the river was filled in and the stone moved. So it's possible that some good soul decided to convert this stone into a stele commemorating the tragic accident.

THE LINOLEUM HOUSE

Åboulevard 84–86, Hans Egede Gade 19–25, Henrik Rung Gade 14–18,
Jesper Brochmands Gade 17, 2200 N
• Metro: Forum

*A piece
of Venice
in Nørrebro*

Designed by the architect Paul Baumann,
the Linoleum House was built by the
City of Copenhagen in 1931. It is the
kind of building you are likely to walk past
without realizing how special it is.

Deeply rooted in Danish architectural history and the Danish brick-laying
tradition, the red and yellow bricks are laid very closely together and create an
attractive soft and rather gentle appearance which is easy on the eye and is in
stark contrast to the rather glaring whiteness of buildings that are part of the
functionalist tradition. The pattern of the coloured bricks, which resembles
that of a 1930s linoleum floor, gave the Linoleum House its name. However,
the architect did not have linoleum in mind when he created his design. As a
young student, Paul Baumann contributed to a survey of Copenhagen's first
Opera House dating from the early 1700s and which is located in the city
centre on the corner of Bredgade and Fredericiagade and whose pattern of
bricks is the model to that of the Linoleum House. In turn, the man behind
the design of the Opera House, the court architect Johan Conrad Ernst, was
inspired by one of the world's greatest architectural feats, namely the diamond-
patterned upper part of the façade of the Doge's Palace in Venice.

> Other buildings in Copenhagen which are also influenced by this Venetian
> style are located at Holbergsgade 3, Bernstorffsgade 3 (the Hercegovina
> restaurant) and in Sankt Peders Stræde 19.

THE STORM P. FRIEZE

Fælledvej 4, 2200 N
Access through the Røde Kors store
• It is advisable to phone beforehand [tel: 35 38 35 48]
• Open 12 noon–4pm weekdays, closed Wednesday
• S-train, Metro: Nørreport

Drinking with Peter Vimmelskaft

In the summer of 1922, on Fælledvej 4 in Inner Nørrebro, the humourist Robert Storm Petersen decorated a small back room with a frieze. It's the last surviving example of this sort of decoration by the hand of Petersen, known as Storm P. - featuring his folk hero, Peter Vimmelskaft. The room was just a small part of a much larger tavern, which stretched up over two floors from the front to the rear of the building. The tavern, named the 'Patricia', stood on this site for twenty-five years. While the other rooms were used as coffee lounges, dining rooms, or for dancing, this little half-concealed room hidden away in the back of the tavern was exclusively used for the serving of alcohol, which probably explains why Storm P. employed drunkenness and general merrymaking as the themes of his frieze.

Storm P. used the good-natured Peter Vimmelskaft, who later became one of his most beloved characters, as the main protagonist in the frieze. In the twenty little adventures that he has, Peter Vimmelskaft is exposed to awful lot: in a scene depicting the Fall of Man, Eve tempts a naked Peter with a bottle of booze – a temptation our alcoholic antihero seems unable to resist. In another little vignette, Storm P. makes his hero "pump" an elephant, and it is hard to imagine that the liquid coming out of the elephant's trunk is alcohol free.

Storm P. borrowed the elephant scene from one used by Fatty Arbuckle, one of the great American silent film stars, who was Peter Vimmelskaft's internationally famous kindred spirit.

The frieze also has a scene where Peter is thrown into prison, and another where he has made himself a cosy bed in the shape of a crescent moon, making sure he still has both a bottle and a glass within easy reach. In a scene of a more satirical nature, the evil Niklas dips Peter in an inkstand. The inkstand bears an inscription which says: "10%". This is a topical reference to an unpopular restaurant tax, which the government had just introduced.

Both Storm P. and Peter Vimmelskaft were two very popular characters, and, throughout his career, Storm P. decorated many other cafés in a similar fashion, but, unfortunately, none of the others has survived. The rear of the building on Fælledvej has only been saved because it was listed as a protected building in the early 1980s.

ROBERT STORM PETERSEN (1882-1949): A FAILED BUTCHER TURNED ARTIST

In a rather unusual career move, Storm P. took up drawing only after failing to become a butcher. Initially, he moved to Paris and then, after working as a cartoonist for the newspaper Ekstra Bladet for many years, he became an entertainer and actor, appearing at the Casino Theatre in Amaliegade and the Dagmar Theatre at the City Hall Square. He then made an unsuccessful attempt to break into films in the U.S.A.; perhaps he was inspired to do this because he admired the silent films of Charlie Chaplin and W.C. Fields, which he'd seen in Copenhagen. Today, he is best known for his ingenious and imaginative Storm P. inventions: surreal contraptions where a simple end result, e.g. making a child swallow a pill, is achieved by the convoluted connection of unlikely objects, people and animals. Storm P. is not so well known for his work as a painter. While his early work was clearly inspired by artists such as Toulouse-Lautrec, Munch and James Ensor, he later found his own naïve style.

The Storm P. Museum, by Frederiksberg Runddel, is also worth a visit.

PETER CHRISTIAN ABILDGAARD'S BURIAL SITE

❺

Assistens Cemetery (*Assistens Kirkegård*), 2200 N
- Access via Kapelvej 2, the Museum Section, Section A
- Open Mon–Sun 7am–10pm (summer); Mon–Sun 7am–7pm (winter)
- Bus 5A, 3A, 350S, 250S

The many-breasted tombstone	In Assistens Cemetery, a rather unusual tombstone showing a many-breasted female figure is dedicated to the natural philosopher and polymath Peter Christian Abildgaard.

Abildgaard was a man of the Enlightenment who was interested in all branches of natural history, as reflected in the carvings. The statue is of the Great Nature Goddess of the Greeks, Artemis of Ephesus, Mother Nature herself … hence the many nurturing breasts.

Underneath the protection of the goddess, the tomb is divided into bands depicting the hierarchy of Nature. The plant kingdom is represented by apple blossom for "Abildgaard" (*abild* means "apple"). Then come insects, butterflies and what are probably little helminths, parasites which live on sticklebacks and which were a particular study of Abildgaard's. Marine creatures come in the guise of a crab accompanied by dolphins; these in turn are followed by the birds, represented by an eagle with outstretched wings. The display is topped off by the mammals in the shape of a ram's head. All lie under the benign protection of Artemis.

However accomplished the tombstone is at conveying Abildgaard's life and oeuvre, it is nevertheless a curious monument. The inspiration for its design may be traced back to one of two different sources: the Renaissance or the Enlightenment, both areas of interest to Abildgaard.

The Renaissance connection might well be with the statue of Artemis that is

part of a spectacular fountain in the Villa d'Este in the Tivoli Gardens in Rome; or perhaps with a similar ancient Roman version in the National Archaeological Museum in Naples, which, in turn, may be a copy of a Greek original.

However, some people think that the idea for the Copenhagen Artemis originated in the philosophies of the Enlightenment and of the French Revolution of 1789, after which, in an attempt to replace traditional religious idols, the figure of Artemis of Ephesus became a symbol of the Philosophy of Nature.

VETERINÆRE

PETER CHRISTIAN ABILDGAARD (1740–1801)

Peter Christian Abildgaard was the older brother of the painter and architect Nicolai Abraham Abildgaard. He was a scientific polymath who trained in medicine and veterinary science. He made a special study of horses and, in 1773, founded the Danish Veterinary School. A mark of his humanity was his invention of a new kind of horseshoe more suited to the animal's physiology. Abildgaard was a man of many interests, including mineralogy, the study of electricity and the development of hot-air balloons, as well as his pioneering use of quarantine to prevent the spread of disease in cattle. We should not, of course, forget his study of the stickleback's parasitic worms. In addition to being a true man of the Enlightenment, Abildgaard founded the Danish Natural History Society in 1789.

HIDDEN SYMBOLISM OF THE STATUE OF ARTEMIS

The rare statues of the Greek goddess Artemis always surprise people with their numerous breasts and animal heads decorating her all-enveloping tunic that reveals only her head, hands and feet, which are black.

The statue actually represents the Great Mother Goddess of the ancient Greeks and later of the Romans, who associated Artemis with the goddess Diana. Hellenic mythology identified Artemis as the daughter of Zeus and

Leto and the twin sister of Apollo. From birth she revealed extraordinary powers in problem-free childbirth – nothing was impossible for the mythological deities. She allegedly helped with the birth of her brother, who represents the Sun, while Artemis is the Moon, as night precedes day. For this reason, the Greeks saw Artemis as the patroness of successful childbirth. She was also worshipped by sterile women trying to get pregnant or young girls praying for an easy delivery, which is why she is represented with her hands outstretched and revealing her many breasts, symbols of fertility.

In addition to her attributes as a heavenly midwife, Artemis was also seen as the "protector of cities" after she protected the temple and the city of Ephesus from a terrible storm that the citizens imputed to other gods, who were jealous of her beauty and gifts. This is why she is often shown, as here, with a tower on her head surrounded by a divine halo, with small faces representing the souls that will spring forth to populate the great cities.

Lastly, Artemis was granted the qualities of a warrior, firing arrows against men who dared to defy her when they infringed Nature, her own creation. She thus became the patron of young animals and women of all ages.

These beliefs led the Romans to invent a new version of Artemis: Diana, literally, "goddess", commonly called "goddess of the hunt" or "protector goddess of hunting", that is, she who offers protection to animal species and to all of Nature, hurling her arrows at misguided men, whom she pursues relentlessly. Diana is represented as a strong young woman with a severe expression, wearing a light tunic revealing legs free to run alongside a doe or a dog. Sometimes she carries a bow and arrow or a torch, and her headdress is a crescent-shaped tiara, another association with the Moon, like Artemis.

Like her brother Apollo, the goddess Artemis was attributed with countless powers. On the one hand, she manifested "benevolent" qualities: she directed the choir of the Muses, uttered oracles, gave good advice, tended illness or injury, protected thermal waters and travel over land or sea and kept an eye on domestic animals and cultivated fields. On the other hand, when confronted, she was the goddess of the hunt for these ignorant men and showed her cruel side, terrorising her prey. She amused herself by oppressing those mortals who defied her, striking them down with epidemics or bringing about violent death. This earned her the nickname "Destroyer".

But for Greeks and Romans alike, Artemis or Diana, "she who evokes the light" (Apollo, the Sun) was above all the Great Mother Goddess, the Goddess of Nature, and her importance was marked by the second day of the week, which the ancients dedicated to the Moon (Monday in English, *Montag* in German, *lunedì* in Italian, *lunes* in Spanish), the "feminine" planet that regulates Nature.

MOSAIC NORTHERN CEMETERY

Møllegade 12, 2200 N
- Open Sun, Mon, Wed & Thurs 10am–6pm
- S-train, Metro: Nørreport

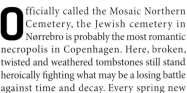

Copenhagen's most romantic necropolis

Officially called the Mosaic Northern Cemetery, the Jewish cemetery in Nørrebro is probably the most romantic necropolis in Copenhagen. Here, broken, twisted and weathered tombstones still stand heroically fighting what may be a losing battle against time and decay. Every spring new vegetation springs up again, especially the tangle of wild strawberries which carpet the ground. But however attractive that might be, it does not stop the soil from piling up higher and higher around the tombs in a slow burial process of its own. Nothing can stop the action of the acid rain and the wind which eat away the surfaces of the limestone and granite, leaving only fragments of tumbled-down, crumbling headstones and fragments and stumps of masonry. There is a Jewish expression, *Beth Ha-Chaim,* meaning "the house of the living". And that's what has happened here: the cemetery has come alive.

Altogether some 6,000 people are buried in the 14,000-m² site. The oldest part, which dates from 1694, contains the graves of Jews who came to Denmark as part of the Diaspora. Here are found the graves of Ashkenazi Jews from Eastern Europe, with stones placed upright at their head. In what is known as the "Portuguese section", there are Sephardic Jews from Spain and Portugal, with the stones lying flat on the ground. The stones carry Hebrew inscriptions, sometimes accompanied by carvings of hands. These are known as the *Kohanim* hands, and they represent the rabbi's gesture of blessing. Another symbol is that of a pitcher pouring water, the pitcher being associated with the Levites, who traditionally washed the hands of the rabbis as part of Jewish religious ritual. In addition, a large, but unknown number of Torah scrolls are buried here as this is the traditional way of disposing of them when they are too worn for further use. The cemetery was closed in 1967 as it was full. In 2011, however, it reopened as a place for local people in need of somewhere to come when they want to escape the noise and bustle of the city.

THE ISLAND OF *FUGLEØEN*

Sortedamssøen, Østerbro
• S-train: Østerport

> *A metropolitan sensation*

In the summer, if you stand beside the shore of the Sortedam Lake and look over to the artificially constructed *Fugleøen* (Bird's Island) you will be witnessing something quite unusual. The island, in the heart of Copenhagen, is the nesting site of a colony of cormorants, whose droppings make a thick white covering for the trees there. It's a unique experience to see them because no other European capital has such a colony of birds right in its centre.

At the beginning of the 1970s the cormorants were near to extinction, because given their notorious reputation for destroying local fish stocks, they were a favourite target for hunters. However, in the 1980s, the cormorants were granted a protection order and around 2000, when their numbers had increased again, they suddenly started nesting on *Fugleøen* in the middle of Copenhagen. In 2012 there were 37 breeding pairs on the island, and, while it is one of the smallest colonies in Denmark, *Fugleøen* is also one of Denmark's smallest islands. The protection of the cormorants is regarded as a success story of Danish nature conservation and the occupation of *Fugleøen* is perhaps the most obvious example of this success.

ANOTHER DRAMATIC OCCUPATION OF *FUGLEØEN*

The cormorants' occupation of *Fugleøen* is not the first in the history of the island. In 1967 a group of anarchists took it over with the aim of drawing attention to America's war in Vietnam. Apart from a small vanguard that had staked it out the night before, the actual occupation took place on the morning of Sunday 29 October. When the island had been captured by 10 so-called freedom fighters, a telegram with a declaration of war was sent off to Lyndon B. Johnson and a membership application made to the UN. The occupation itself was celebrated with a salute fired from heavy firecrackers and the letting off of fireworks. Freedom banners were raised and a vote on the composition and policies of the island's future anarchist government was held. In spite of the light-hearted way in which the occupation was conducted, the political context was serious enough. For a brief moment, the occupiers caused Denmark and its NATO allies to feel rather nervous.

JOHAN HANSEN EXHIBITION BUILDING

Museumsbygningen
Kastelvej 18, 2100 Østerbro
• Open Tues–Sat 12am–4pm
• S-train: Østerport

Extensions to a dream

Wedged between two large residential blocks on Kastelvej, today the former Johan Hansen Exhibition Building is a gallery (*Banja Rathnov Galleri og Kunsthandel*). In fact, the building consists of two different wings; one carries a tight architectural decoration, the other is plain and free of decoration.

In 1915 Johan Hansen – Consul General, ship-owner and politician – bought one of the city's finest houses, built in the late 1800s by Martin Nyrop, the architect of Copenhagen City Hall. The following year Hansen built an annexe, connected to the villa by a winter garden, where he installed a large art collection and opened it to the public. He wanted to create an exhibition space for less well-known Danish painters, even though one room was devoted to the works of the famous Danish landscape artist, Johan Thomas Lundbye.

In 1920, keen to expand his exhibition space, Hansen added an extension to the original gallery, at the same time facilitating public access via an entrance on Kastelvej. Despite their differences, the two buildings blend harmoniously as they are the work of the same architects, Poul J. Methling and Einar Madvig.

The collection came to a sad end, however. Only a few years after the last extension, the family business – the C. K. Hansen shipping company – was on the point of collapse: the days of the collection were numbered and in 1932, when the situation got worse, Johan Hansen had to let it go. The paintings were distributed between a number of Danish galleries where you can still view them.

In 1936 even Nyrop's villa was demolished to make way for the neighbouring functionalistic white building dating from 1938. Today only the two extensions remain, in memory of Hansen's broken dream.

BUTCHER'S FRIEZE

Rosenvængets Allé 7A, 2100 Ø
- Access within normal shop opening hours
- Bus 1A

> *The city's most beautiful butcher's shop*

In the heart of Østerbro, in what is the city's most beautiful butcher's shop, there's a 100-year-old frieze which shows a little bit of Danish history and is fun to look at. In cartoon style, it shows how meat is processed, from cows standing in a field to becoming steak on the butcher's counter. The artist is unknown, but it might be the work of painter Erik Henningsen, who was known as a popular portrayer of Copenhagen life. Today, he is best known for having created *Tuborgmanden*, a famous poster that he designed in 1900 to advertise the Tuborg brewery.

The cartoons in the frieze show scenes from the life of a butcher, his wife and his assistants as well as the fate of the animals. It begins with the picture of a cow and her newborn calf standing in an idyllic Danish pasture. Next, a parade of cows is shown going off to the butchers' halls. Other panels display further scenes in the cycle until finally, the jolly butcher, in his white jacket and bow tie, is shown selling the meat from his well-stocked shop to happy customers, while his wife sits behind the counter keeping accounts and counting the cash.

For many years, the Butcher's Frieze was all but forgotten. Not until 1999, when one of Østerbro's old neighbourhood pubs moved out, did it show up again. The dirt coating the ceiling was hiding the original brass-mounted glass panels, and layers of worn carpets had concealed the original white tiles. But most important of all, from under several layers of wallpaper, the painted frieze came to light. Experts were called in and found that the decorations dated from around 1900, when a butcher had moved into the premises. However, in 1908, the old butcher's shop closed and it subsequently became home to several pubs and, at one point, a hairdresser's. With each new owner and each new layer of wallpaper, the frieze slipped further into oblivion, until it was uncovered some 100 years later. For some years there was a café there, but in 2007 a new butcher moved in, thus closing the circle.

IDRÆTSHUSET PICTOGRAMS ⑩

Østerbro Stadium (formerly Copenhagen Sports Park)
Gunnar Nu Hansens Plads 7, 2100 Ø
• Bus 1A

Precursors of Olympic pictograms

The premises of the former Copenhagen Sports Park offer so many attractions that the sporting pictograms on the *Idrætshuset* façade are not necessarily the first thing you notice. Like all symbols, they consist of simple shapes and lines: square, rectangle, lozenge or circle which, depending on their juxtaposition, form an image with sporting connotations.

Idrætshuset was built to host major gymnastic competitions, with four smaller halls designed for wrestling, boxing, fencing and dancing: the five sports represented by the pictograms.

These symbols, designed in 1914 as a nice addition to the decoration of the façade, predate those of the Berlin Olympics of 1936: although pictograms were used at the Berlin Games, they were not widespread until the London Olympics of 1948. They reappeared in Tokyo in 1964, but they found their most emblematic expression in the timeless creations of the German designer Otl Aicher for the 1972 Munich Games.

Idrætshuset, built by the architect Søren Lemche (1864–1955) and the engineer Edouard Suenson (1877–1958), is a large multi-sports stadium in reinforced concrete, the first use of this material on such a scale in Denmark. The six giant arches that support the roof of the building are also worth a look.

FAÇADE
OF NYBORGGADE TRANSFORMER STATION

Nyborggade 13, 2100 Ø
• Access: visits to the interior of the building are not permitted
• S-train: Svanemøllen

> *The poetry
> of cheap
> materials*

The architect Hans Christian Hansen is probably unknown to the general public, but go out to Nyborggade, where his 1960 transformer station is located next to the more famous *Østre Gasværk* building, and you will discover an example of a type of 20th-century Danish architecture that has been rather overlooked – the poetry of cheap materials.

Here, Hansen reinterprets P. V. Jensen-Klint's Grundtvig's Church at Bispebjerg: the expressive power is the same, vertical and neo-Gothic, but the materials are completely different. Few people would imagine that cheap industrial pressure-treated timber fixed to reinforced concrete, and the use of asphalt roofing, could replace expensive Danish brick and result in such a powerful, beautiful piece of architecture. The sloping roofs, covered with wooden shingles, are in the Nordic Romantic tradition and the influence of Norwegian stave churches is unmistakable.

The 1960s saw an explosion in the cost of building materials, and Hansen made it his mission to search for beauty on the cheap. Most of his works employed Eternit (a fibre cement material) as their basis, which resulted in constructions of a poetic beauty. Another of Hansen's fine industrial buildings is the Svanemølle converter station (1968), which is located behind the transformer station.

OTHER BUILDINGS BY HANS CHRISTIAN HANSEN (1901–78)

Other buildings in Copenhagen designed by Hansen include: the converter station at Bellahøj on Hulgårdsvej; the inner-city Bremerholm transformer station next to the Magasin department store; the Amager converter station on Irlandsvej; the expansion of the Gasværksvejens School on Vesterbro; and Tagensbo Church in outer Nørrebro.

TUBERCULOSIS SHEDS

Ved Sporsløjfen, 2100 Ø
• S-train: Svanemøllen

With the coastal railway behind the headboard

lose to the railway line next to Svanemøllen Station stands an impressive row of wooden sheds that follow the line of the rail track. Your first thought is that they must be old stock-sheds for the State railways. They are not.

Located in the backyard of the former Øresund Hospital, which closed in 1982, these sheds were actually used for the treatment of tuberculosis patients for more than seventy years. In early spring, well tucked up under several layers of blankets, the patients could rest here, in the open air. The sheds face south-west and as they were open at the front in those days, patients could benefit from sitting out in the sunshine.

The Øresund Hospital opened in 1878 as a quarantine and epidemic hospital for the municipality of Copenhagen. At that time, this was a rural stretch of land, far outside the city, located right on the coast. Originally, the hospital worked exclusively with the treatment of diseases such as smallpox and cholera. It even had its own jetty, so that naval personnel who had been infected abroad could be taken straight from their ships to the hospital. However, this practice ceased when the hospital lost its direct access to the shore after the coastal railway was built in 1897. Later, in 1905, it was rebuilt as a hospital specialising in the treatment of tuberculosis and so the sheds probably date from that time.

In the 19th century, tuberculosis was rampant in Denmark and many people in the densely populated areas of Copenhagen fell victim to the disease. Well into the 20th century, the treatment consisted primarily of a healthy diet combined with plenty of sunshine and fresh air. The rich went to the French Riviera or to a spa in Central Europe, but most of the locals had to settle for a trip to the sheds in Østerbro.

FRITZ KOCH-DESIGNED TELEPHONE KIOSK ⓭

Poul Henningsen Plads, 2100 Østerbro
• S-train: Svanemøllen

New images for the new city

The Copenhagen telephone kiosk is a beautiful example of the sort of urban design which evolved around 1900. The hexagonal structure has carved wooden panels, which in addition to displaying the twelve signs of the zodiac also show images of flora and fauna as well as shipping and telecommunications. Every space is crammed with eclectic small details, such as a giant octopus and a bunch of little jellyfish swimming alongside a Chinese figure and a couple of Mohawk braves.

The kiosk was designed by the architect Fritz Koch, who, in 1896, was given the task by the KTK Company (Copenhagen Telephone Kiosks). The challenge of designing a small structure to make Graham Bell's 1870 invention accessible to a larger audience, however, also demanded finding suitable imagery and symbols to reflect the spirit of the new technology. Originally, the kiosks were manned and, in addition to selling phone calls, they also sold newspapers and stamps. The little buildings – based on a French model – were also fitted with advertising posters whose execution was entrusted to an artist. The work was done to a very high standard and the response from a (usually critical) Copenhagen audience was extremely positive. A contemporary commentator wrote: "The kiosks on our streets are of an infinitely higher quality than those you see in places of this sort in other capital cities.

The people of Copenhagen should be told to take notice of these kiosks with their fine and graceful details and not to rush by them, too busy to give them a second glance."

That was the favourable verdict in 1905, at a time when the kiosks had only been in business for ten years. It certainly still holds true today.

For many years, Fritz Koch's (1857–1905) telephone kiosks could be seen on all the busiest streets and squares of Copenhagen. Unfortunately, over time, most of them have disappeared, but you can still see them in a few places. Besides the one in Østerbro, kiosks can also be found in the city centre in Kultorvet square and in the little square at the corner of Fiolstræde and Nørrevoldgade. In the Vesterbro neighbourhood, there is a kiosk on Absalonsgade; in Nørrebro, there is one in Sankt Hans Torv square; and in Christianshavn, there is one in Christianshavn Torv square. For still more kiosks, try your luck in Tivoli and Bakken.

BAT WALKS IN FÆLLEDPARKEN

Fælledparken, 2100 Ø
- Miljøpunkt Østerbro arranges bat walks in Fælledparken
- www.miljopunktosterbro.wordpress.com

> **With a bevy of hunting mammals over your head**

A couple of times during the season, Miljøpunkt Østerbro organizes very interesting "bat walks" in Fælledparken. Bats are famous for their use of ultrasound, the excrement they leave in the old trees where they live and their precisely timed activities – you could almost set your watch by them as they start their night shift at exactly the same time every evening. But bats are also famous for being one of Copenhagen's most invisible inhabitants.

The walk nearly always manages to be at the right spot when the common noctule bats synchronize their nightly hunt for insects. This means that, for a few minutes at least, you'll probably have up to 50 hungry little creatures with a wingspan of 40 centimetres flapping above your head.

Afterwards, the walk heads towards the lakes in the park where the Daubenton's bats can be seen chasing insects over the lake at breakneck speed. Besides the common noctule and the Daubenton's bat you can also see the parti-coloured bat in the Fælledparken. This is a decidedly urban bat, the population in North Seeland, including Copenhagen, being considered to be the world's densest. During the summer, the creature stays in the countryside, but as autumn approaches, it gravitates to the city with its tall buildings to find a place for the winter. These buildings serve as a substitute for their former habitat in sea cliffs where they would go to mate and have their young; so if you listen carefully in autumn, you will hear the male's mating call. These bats make good use of the urban environment in other ways as well. For example, they use the city lampposts as virtual food dispensers: the swarms of insects, which are attracted to the light in the late summer evenings and at night, provide the bats with a ready source of fast food.

The bat is a protected species in virtually all European countries, but that alone is not enough. It is also important to protect its habitats, such as old trees and the other nooks and crannies where they make their homes. For this reason, the City of Copenhagen is committed to providing special protection to five species of bat: the parti-coloured, the common noctule, the Daubenton's, the Nathusius' pipistrelle, and the soprano pipistrelle, all of which are included in the municipality's biodiversity programmes.

WHALE BASEMENT

Zoological Museum, Universitetsparken 15, 2100 Ø
- Access: tours can be arranged with the Zoological Museum
(tel: 35 32 22 22)
- Bus 150S, 18

An amazing final resting place for whales

Under the Zoological Museum, a large garage door leads to an old basement car park. Go through a plastic curtain there and you will come to what is one of the finest and oldest collections of whales in the world. The first thing to strike you is an acrid smell of whale oil, something that will follow you throughout your entire visit.

The basement is packed with huge skeletons of whales (humpbacks, fin or finbacks and sperm whales) that have either been stranded in Danish waters or killed in the North Atlantic over the last 200 years. In the 19th century, whaling in the Northern hemisphere was big business and fortunes were made from extracting the oil, which was used to fuel the street lamps in Europe's growing cities.

The bleached skeletons lie side by side: rib by rib and skull by skull. It is as if you are looking at an exposed cemetery. It is not at all gruesome, however; rather, it is eerily beautiful and somewhat overwhelming. The shape and texture of the bones give them the appearance of ceramic artworks or slices of smooth concrete. You might be in a modern art gallery. But the whale basement is not just the final resting place of these giants of the sea: it is also a learning experience for all those who want to know more about these amazing marine mammals. You'll be allowed to hold an ear bone, see the eyes of a blue whale – eyes which are big as saucers – floating in a glass container of formaldehyde, and get a close-up view of huge whale skulls which resemble creatures from outer space. It's an amazing, rather surreal, experience. Even more mind-blowing is the size of these creatures. The skeleton of a blue whale, which was stranded in Årøsund in 1931, is 24 m long and stretches from the back of the basement right through the entire length of the building. It lies next to what is reckoned to be the oldest specimen of a fin whale in the world: it was stranded in Vejle Fjord in 2010 and is estimated to be between 120 and 130 years old.

The whale collection was founded by the zoologist and pioneer Daniel Frederik Eschricht (1798–1863), who started collecting whale skeletons in Copenhagen in the 19th century. At first he stored them in his own house in Badstuestræde. Then, in 1841, the university bought his collection and the skeletons were placed in the basement of its banqueting hall at Vor Frue Plads. In the 1970s, they were moved to the newly built Zoological Museum. For incomprehensible reasons, a separate exhibition hall was never built for the whales, so they have had to settle for a disused underground car park.

SHOCK CONCRETE OF OSRAM HOUSE

Valhalsgade 4, 2200 N
• Bus 6A

*A house
that deserves
to be caressed*

Situated in a quiet side street off busy Tagensvej in a part of Nørrebro mostly frequented by locals, Osram House is one of Copenhagen's most remarkable buildings, though even its famous neon sign has not stopped it being one of the most overlooked.

Built in 1952–53 by the architect Charles Weidemann Petersen (1907–73) at the request of the founder of Danish Osram, the businessman Søren Madsen, Osram House was one of the first in Denmark to be built of shock concrete – at that time, a cutting-edge technology in concrete construction.

The technique was originally developed in the Netherlands, where it achieved widespread popularity during the 1930s. The production method is simple: the concrete elements of the building are pre-cast in moulds on a "blasting" table. This is then used to compress the concrete more tightly and, in turn, causes a reduction in the air bubbles and the water content of the mix. This manufacturing process results in a concrete that is far more durable than that made by other methods. Other characteristics of shock concrete are its density and its glassy surface, a feature that you might want to test: with its smooth surfaces, Osram House is indeed a building to be touched and caressed.

The shock-concrete method also gave architects the freedom to be more innovative in their designs: the moulds in which the concrete was cast posed almost no limits to the imagination. The architect of Osram House himself considered that the greatest danger of using this technique was the tendency to become too frivolous in terms of design. And he predicted that further development of the method would result in a variety of strange architectural shapes. Nevertheless, you cannot accuse his building of being frivolous in any way: it is simple and beautiful. Its square-patterned windows, with their vertical slats, capture light and shadow at different hours of the day in a very attractive way.

Danish Osram remained in the building until 1980. In 2009 it was renovated as part of the COP15 climate summit and, since the summer of 2010, it has served as a local cultural centre. This means that the door is almost always open for you to look around and see the interior.

ASTRID NOACK'S STUDIO

Rådmandsgade 34, 2200 N
• The studio opens to the public for special events (see www.astrid-noack.dk)
• Bus 6A

> *The modest workplace of a hard-working artist*

On Rådmandsgade, a small dilapidated building facing onto the street hides a little passage that takes you to an authentic 19th-century Nørrebro backyard that has survived both demolition and the general gentrification. Originally a stable, the place boasts a row of old garages with red wooden doors; an even smaller yard lies behind. All the roofs are uneven, which only adds to the cluttered charm of the place.

In 1936, the sculptor Astrid Noack (1888–1954) moved into the old stable and set up a simple studio, where she lived and worked until 1950. This is where she produced some of her best-loved sculptures, which today have made her the only woman recognised in the official canon of Danish art.

A small memorial plaque on the façade commemorates Noack's work on the site. When she first settled here, this backyard was a vibrant working-class neighbourhood. The building at the front housed a tobacco shop and a small apartment, and the backyard was home to poor people who lived alongside a saddler's workshop and a pastry bakery.

Noack was originally from Ribe; after training as a sculptor at Vallekilde School College, she moved to Copenhagen in 1910. She then worked there

for several years before settling in Paris after the First World War. Her talent blossomed in the French capital with its bustling artistic community. However, after the Great Crash of 1929, she returned to Denmark.

The workers' environment and the people in Rådmandsgade reminded her of her time in Paris and, although she was honoured with scholarships and received some payment for her sculptures, she lived the rest of her life very modestly.

Founded in 2009, the Association ANA (Astrid Noacks Atelier) aims at preserving the studio itself as well as the backyard environment of which it is a part. ANA opens the studio periodically when special events are held there.

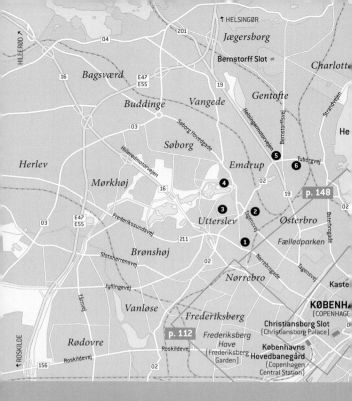

OUTSIDE THE CENTRE NORTH

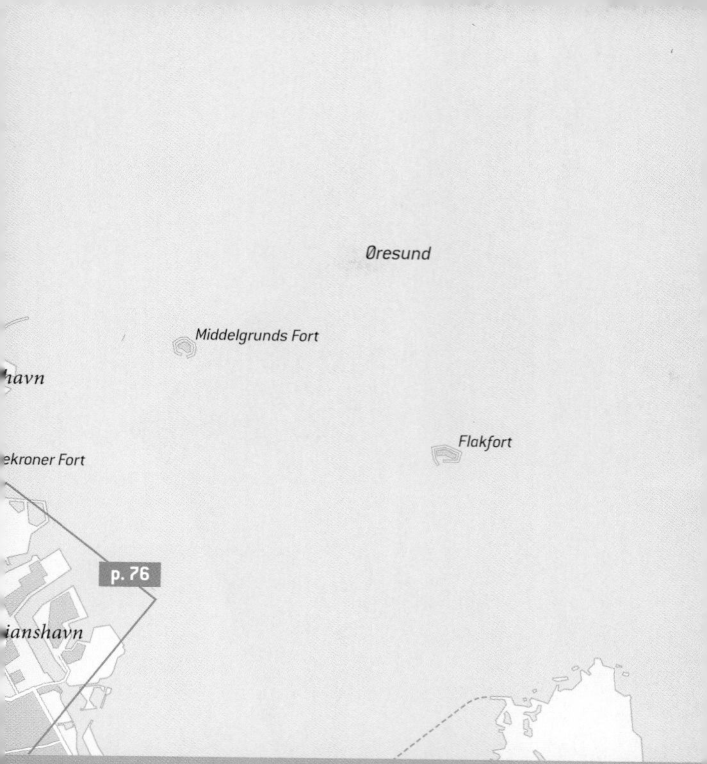

Øresund

Middelgrunds Fort

havn

Flakfort

ekroner Fort

p. 76

ianshavn

SJAKKET BUILDING

Skaffervej 4-6, 2400 NV
• Bus 4A

> *Under the rafters of an old wagon shed*

At first glance, the Sjakket building is just another typical example of the architectural legacy left in the north-west by the many small, early 20th-century industries which are now defunct.

The two halves of the building, which sit side by side, are not, at first glance, of any great interest. People usually need a reason to explore them. However, go through the gates, which are often open, and you will find that the site is deceptive – it is actually interesting and full of activity.

Behind the building, a steep staircase leads to the roof terrace – the so-called "cleavage" – which gets its name from the space between the two semicircular roofs. As you make your way up, a giant red container floats above your head, resting playfully on the top of the roof. The container is actually a music studio, whereas one half of the building below contains small offices. The other half is multi-purpose, with space and seating for sports events and concerts.

This idiosyncratic twin-roofed building was constructed in 1938 as the production site of an ink factory. Interestingly, the rafters were recycled from a former royal wagon shed near Hellerup Station. When the ink factory closed, the building was turned into a garage. Then, in 1996, Sjakket moved into the premises.

Sjakket – meaning "team of builders" – is a private foundation working to improve conditions for the local children. The building was totally renovated between 2004 and 2007 in an attempt to create new life under the old rafters. The firm of architects behind the renovation was PLOT, led by Julien de Smidt and Bjarke Ingels, who was then quite unknown. Ingels' firm BIG has since become famous for the design of some outstanding buildings in Copenhagen's Ørestad, namely, the Mountain Dwellings and the Figure of 8 House.

THE TUNNEL SYSTEM UNDER BISPEBJERG HOSPITAL ❷

Bispebjerg Hospital
Bispebjerg Bakke 23, 2400 NV
• S-train: Bispebjerg or Emdrup, Bus 6A, 69, 21, 42 or 43

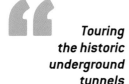

Touring the historic underground tunnels

A visit to the underground corridor system under Bispebjerg Hospital is simply a great experience: at first, it takes a little courage to venture down into these working regions of the hospital, but soon you'll just enjoy the sheer engineering achievement which has created this seemingly endless maze. Since almost all of the buildings in the hospital grounds are interconnected by way of the tunnels, in principle, you can just choose any of them; go down to the basement and begin your underground adventure from there. But, bear in mind that the hospital is a workplace, therefore visitors should behave accordingly. The best time to visit is at weekends after 5 p.m. when you will almost certainly have the place to yourself.

Martin Nyrop, the architect of the Copenhagen City Hall, completed Bispebjerg Hospital in 1913. It was built in accordance with the medical philosophy current at that time, i.e. constructing freestanding pavilions in the middle of an immense garden to provide the two main conditions for healing: sunlight and fresh air. And everything that could be a potential nuisance was hidden in the 5.5 km-long tunnel system. Apart from ensuring a practical and sheltered access route between the pavilions, which was used for the transport of patients, food and clothing, the tunnels also served as the conduit for all the heating and electricity services.

When it was completed, the hospital consisted of six pavilions for patients, an administration building, a bathhouse, a kitchen, a laundry and the nurses' quarters. In addition to being interconnected by underground corridors, these building were also connected to the central services hub. From there, all the main pipes from the boiler and machine rooms distributed steam, hot water and electricity throughout the building.

THE TUNNELS AS A PLACE OF SAFETY IN WARTIME

In August 1943 the Danish policy of cooperation (*samarbejdspolitikken*) with the German occupiers broke down, and, in the wake of this, the Germans began to direct their attention towards the Danish Jews, who had hitherto avoided deportation to the concentration camps in Germany. On the night of 2 October, the great plan designed to rescue Denmark's Jewish citizens was put into operation. Several hospitals around the country, including Bispebjerg, were chosen to serve as meeting points for the Jewish people before they made their final escape to Sweden across the Øresund Sound. It is estimated that approximately two thousand refugees came to the hospital during the month of October 1943. Among other places, they were hidden in the many underground rooms located in the hospital's tunnel system. From these, the Jews were smuggled out in ambulances and even in coffins, as part of mock funeral processions.

CHERRY TREES AT BISPEBJERG KIRKEGÅRD ❸

Bispebjerg Kirkegård, 2400 NV
Access via Støvnæs Allé
• Bus 250S, 350S

*Blanketed
in pink*

Few Copenhageners are aware that every year at Bispebjerg Kirkegård you can witness a little piece of Japanese theatre. It is usually around Easter but this, of course, depends on when spring arrives. As in Japan, it is important to be on the spot as this spectacular sight seldom lasts more than a week – then the heavy pink blanket is gone.

The botanical name for the trees at Bispebjerg is *Prunus subhirtella "Autumnalis"*, the winter-flowering cherry. This type of cherry tree is known for producing an enormous number of flowers in spring, when its branches are a mass of pink blossoms. It is, however, named after its somewhat more subdued relative, which blooms in autumn and winter as long as the weather is mild and the trees still have buds. The tree is a cultivar and not found in the wild; it is thought to have originated in Japan.

For the Japanese, there is no surer sign of spring than the blooming of the cherry trees, the so-called *sakura*. We Westerners have warm fronts and cold fronts, but the Japanese have an additional *sakura*-front. The Japanese National Meteorological Institute keeps a close eye on it as it moves northwards: starting in the south in January and ending in the north in April. The *sakura* includes *hanami* – the act of enjoying a picnic under the blooming cherry tree. At Bispebjerg, there is every opportunity for both Copenhageners and visitors to copy this tradition.

ATELIERHUSENE

Grønnemose Allé 21–47, 2400 NV
• www.atelierhusene.dk
• Open once a year, usually the second Sunday in September
• Bus 6A

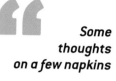

Some thoughts on a few napkins

I n September, the community of artists who live and work at the *Atelierhusene* celebrate its annual Open Doors event. It is just as much about a social gathering of families, friends, colleagues and acquaintances as it is about art. So if you think you are there only to look at architecture and art, think again: you have really landed in the middle of a big family celebration where you will be warmly welcomed with a smile as well as with food and drink. In many of the 21 houses you will not only be invited into the studio, but into the living room and out into the back garden too.

The event is very popular: Open Doors Day is the only chance that the public has to have a look at this piece of outstanding architecture designed by Viggo Møller-Jensen (1907–2003), who also gave his name to the lake at the back of some of the houses.

With a couple of sculptor friends he conceived the idea for the development when he was teaching at the art academy: artists in the city required a new place to work because the artists' home in Gothersgade dated from 1878 and no longer met their requirements. Møller-Jensen actually drew the first sketches for it on a napkin in the academy canteen in 1941. After that, the project quickly got the necessary support and it was finished in 1943.

In architectural circles, the *Atelierhusene* has become a point of reference for its imaginative construction and for the way simple, basic materials were used to aesthetically pleasing effect. It was also commended for its clever and effective use of natural light, so essential for artists' studios, and for the intelligent planning of the interiors where form follows function. The way the houses are set in the landscape is also remarkable, and attractive too, as the buildings seem to have become almost a natural part of the area around the lakeside.

The people who are lucky enough to live here really *are* living the artist's dream: their workplaces and homes are side by side, rents are low and they are all part of one community where they can share both ideas and friendships.

DANISH SHOE MUSEUM

5

Vespervej 40, 2900 Hellerup
- Access by special appointment with *Kjøbenhavns Skomagerlaug*
- Tel: 43 96 64 04 or 51 18 21 40
- Admission: 25 DKK
- Bus 150S, 184, 21

A hidden paradise for fashion lovers

From the outside, the Danish Shoe Museum doesn't look like anything much as it's located in an anonymous street and hidden away in a basement. However, a guided tour is a wonderful journey through the history of the shoe trade and a fascinating look at the history of fashion itself. Founded in 1934, the museum is run by the *Kjøbenhavns Skomagerlaug* (the Copenhagen Shoemakers Guild) which was founded in 1509 after the shoemaking trade and its techniques developed during the 15th and 16th centuries. The oldest shoes in the museum, which were found during an archaeological excavation in Copenhagen, date from the 18th century. The

display of 19th-century shoes is quite a parade of different styles, including: delicate silk bootees, high heeled *sudersko* used by sailors, slim side-buttoned shoes with pointed toes, white lace-up boots, cool elastic-sided Chelsea boots, and lots and lots of French heels. There's also a whole display case with footwear produced as part of the Danish exhibition at the Paris *Exposition Universelle* in 1889 – the year that the Eiffel Tower was built and black and yellow shoes were apparently in vogue.

The coming of industrialization in the early 20th century meant that the shoemaking trade's later years saw an increasingly fierce battle for the survival of the old craft. However, manufacturers like Hertz, Panther, Darmer and Würtzen did manage to keep the bespoke industry alive, despite competition from a flood of cheap imports.

The museum documents this survival in its collection of 20th-century shoes. There's a wealth of examples on display: classic men's dress shoes, brogues, stylish women's shoes with decorated heels, riding boots, golf shoes, patent leather shoes, and – as one of the highlights – the world-famous Wagner tenor Lauritz Melchior's thigh-high safari boots.

Today, the craft has survived mainly due to the work of orthopaedic shoemakers, which ensures that people with disabilities, who need specially adapted footwear, can still be both dignified and fashionable.

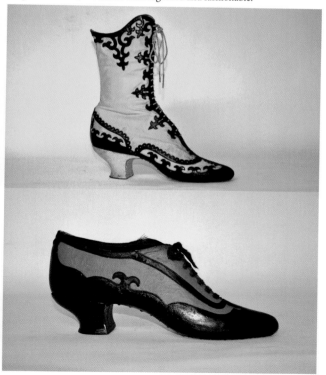

DANSK TENNIS CLUB

6

Rygårds Allé 73–75, 2900 Hellerup
• Open from 1 Sep until 30 Apr
• The court can be rented by contacting Eva Sehested
• Tel: 39 61 00 84 • sehested@hotmail.com
• S-train: Hellerup

The response of a banned tennis champion

North of the city, where only a few Copenhageners ever go, is a building of unusual quality, an example of magnificent 1920s architecture. As soon as you enter you become aware of its unique character: Egyptian wall decorations continue throughout the building, which is home to a beautiful tennis court. The tops of the walls are lined with windows which have large white canvas screens shielding the court from too much sun. The atmosphere here is quiet, serene even; the brightest colour is the green baize of the court surfaces which is complemented by the dark ochre used on the end walls and the oxblood red woodwork. On the side of the court facing the garden there are double doors opening onto the outside, and, on the opposite side, other doors give access to the tearoom.

The person behind this great place was Leif Sadi Rovsing, who was one of Denmark's greatest tennis celebrities in the early 1900s. In 1910 he played at Wimbledon, and, in 1912, he represented Denmark at the Olympics in Sweden. He also had several Danish championship titles to his name. In 1917, however, his world collapsed. The Danish Ball Game Association – *Dansk Boldspil Union* – expelled him for his homosexuality, and, at the same time, he was banned from participation in all tournaments.

In response to this, he founded his own *Dansk Tennis Club* in 1919, and, in 1921, he built the arena, which he deliberately called a "World Sports Establishment". It was one of Copenhagen's first indoor tennis arenas, and, today, it stands as a testament to the fate of Leif Rovsing. On his death in 1977, he left behind not just the building, but also a large fortune, which helps to ensure the continued existence of the club.

OUTSIDE THE CENTRE
SOUTH

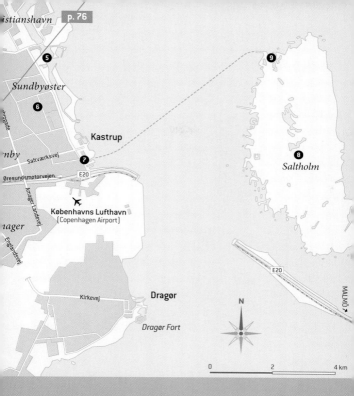

Kastrup

København Lufthavn
(Copenhagen Airport)

Dragør

Dragør Fort

Saltholm

Kirkevej

Sundbyøster

nby

Saltværksvej

Øresundsmotorvejen

Amager Landevej

E20

Englandsvej

nager

N

E20

MALMÖ

0   2   4 km

COPENHAGEN FIRE MUSEUM

Brandstation Dæmningen
Hansstedvej 7, 2. sal, 2500 Valby
• www.kbhbrandmuseum.dk
• Open Tues 1pm–4pm
• Admission: free
• S-train: Hvidovre, Danshøj

> **A museum that's well worth seeking out**

Visitors entering the fascinating Copenhagen Fire Museum are welcomed by one of the museum's volunteers, but don't be surprised if the first thing they ask you is how you managed to get there in the first place. Apparently, it has so few visitors that it's a bit of a shock to them when people do actually find it!

Like all densely populated cities, Copenhagen has a long history of city fires that have led to real tragedies, as in 1728 and again in 1795.

The museum documents the history of firefighting in Copenhagen. On display are images of horse-drawn carriages, the story of the first fire engine dating from 1907, the first telegraph of 1860, 18th-century hand pumps, photos of one of the great steam pumps that brewery owner Carl Jacobsen donated to the fire brigade; and an interesting collection of firefighters' masks.

One of the most striking objects is a model of the Bernstorff House in Bredgade, made by firefighters for the Nordic Industrial, Agricultural and Art Exhibition in Copenhagen in 1888. It shows how a fire would have been dealt with at that time. You can see the speedy horse-driven fire engines arriving, along with the wagon carrying the ladder, the setting up of the pressure hoses and – the highlight of the tableau – a group of firefighters holding a blanket, ready to catch a man who is about to jump down from the roof.

Another point of interest: the visit is normally guided by dedicated volunteers, former or current employees of the fire brigade, which means that, whatever stories they tell, there is always a personal twist to them.

THE SYDHAVNSTIPPEN

Copenhagen South Harbour (Sydhavnen)
Access either via Valbyparken or the small gravel road at the bottom of
Sydløbsvej
• Bus 4A

Archaeologist for a day

I
f you want to do a little excavating, start from the centre of Copenhagen, go by bike to Sluseholmen and continue on over the bridge along Fiskerihavnen until you reach the bottom of Bådehavnsgade, where a little dirt road, called Sydløbsvej, leads to Valbyparken. On your left-hand side, behind a fence, you'll see a large attractive-looking grassy area scattered with a few trees. Go through one of the little gates and you will suddenly find yourself in a totally different world, where sheep are grazing and winding paths take you through a landscape of blackberry bushes, apple trees and little mysterious grassy mounds.

This world is called *Tippen* (from the Danish word *tippe*, meaning to unload). It gets its name from the thousands of trucks that, from 1950 until well into the 1980s, tipped their loads of rubble and other Copenhagen waste onto this site.

Tippen is a paradise built on top of five-metre-high piles of rubbish, and the strange little grassy hills, some of which look like miniature barrows, are basically just piles of rubbish, hiding everything from construction waste to worn-out shoes. Here and there you may come across a rusty old bed, a discarded tombstone or the rusting pipes of old plumbing equipment sticking out of the ground.

Tippen has proved a huge asset to the locals, who have made great efforts to maintain and develop the land so that today it serves as a unique recreation area, which is abundant in wildlife. In 1990, the southernmost part of *Tippen* was protected and in 2009 the area got a nature school to the delight of the many children's institutions in Copenhagen.

However, many Copenhageners still do not know anything at all about the existence of *Tippen*, and the area contains many secrets even for the locals. For example, on the east-facing coast, the porcelain manufacturer Royal Copenhagen has disposed of huge quantities of old moulds and lots of broken cups, bowls and plates from their Aluminia production line, which closed down in 1969. It is therefore possible to be an archaeologist for a day, scraping your finds out from the layers in the mounds, one potsherd after another.

BÅDKLUBBEN VALBY

Oscar Pettifords Vej 10, 2450 SV
• Kitchen open weekends 10am–4pm
• S-train: Sydhavn

> *A nice
> old boatclub
> saved by
> a Dutch architect*

Although *Bådklubben Valby* (the Valby Boat Club) is a private club, don't let that stop you dropping by to enjoy a beer or a meal. It's a friendly place with affordable prices and, in summer, it's a real pleasure to sit outdoors, where you can enjoy the view of the Sluseholm area.

Bådklubben Valby is a motorboat club, which currently has eighty-five berths for motorboats and twenty-four for kayaks. If you are interested in becoming a member however, you should be prepared to be put on a very long waiting list. The club was founded in the mid 1970s by a group of taxi drivers from Valby – hence the name. It was previously located closer to the city centre and, around 2000, it escaped being a victim of the redevelopment of the Sluseholm area. It was saved by the Dutch architect Sjoerd Soeters, who was invited to create a master plan for the area and who insisted on keeping the club. So, thanks to him, Copenhageners can now not only enjoy a beer in the sun, but also appreciate the contrast between the homely old boat club and the newly built, and still a little sterile, canal city.

PET CEMETERY

❹

Glamsbjergvej 5, 2720 Kastrup
- Call 38 88 16 93 before visiting
- Open Tues–Thurs 10am–2pm
- Ørestadstog Tårnby

The last resting place of family pets

I n a normally quiet residential street of Copenhagen, 700 graves are dotted around a rather unusual cemetery where the dead are interred in miniature coffins and urns. The graves are alongside paths bordered by small and well-maintained boxwood hedges: everything is on a similar scale to Legoland or any other Lilliputian place. Even the benches where you can sit and relax are more suitable for small people.

This is in fact a pet cemetery where thousands of animals – cats, dogs, guinea pigs, birds and rats – are buried under tombstones with inscriptions such as: "Thank you for your faithfulness", "My best friend, thank you for everything", "I love you and miss you", "Sweet dreams, our little girl". Many of these graves contain several animals belonging to the same person.

The small graves are also decorated with animal figurines, candles and flowers or sometimes toys that the animals used to play with. A Pekingese dog even has its own mausoleum, while a group of rats is buried under a wooden house that was once in their cage.

At one end of the cemetery, Marianne, the sexton, has a wooden hut where she can store tools and enjoy a cup of coffee and a smoke. Since 1989, when her dog was buried here, Marianne has done voluntary work that involves digging, trimming hedges, weeding and officiating at funerals. She always ensures that the animals' heads are facing in the same direction so that their souls may rise with the Sun in the east. She also advises people on their choice of appropriate tombstones and lends a patient ear to the many stories owners tell about their pets.

This job has given her a profound knowledge of the graves: she is happy to show visitors where the famous dog Kvik – star of the TV series *Matador* – is buried, as well as another grave where a woman places the dead birds she collects in the street, or even the five or six graves reserved by young men for their muscular dogs.

The pet cemetery was founded in 1949 by businessman A. C. Andersen, who had acquired the land. Today the cemetery is managed by a board of 600 members, all of whom have an animal buried here. For a modest sum, anyone can bury their animals in one of these little graves. Only animals like monkeys and reptiles or animals larger than dogs are not catered for.

LITTLE HELGOLAND

Access from Amager Strandvej via Vågestien towards the shore
• Metro: Lergravsparken

> *The permanent temporary bathhouse*

Just north of Amager Beach, at the end of a jetty, close to the *Søstjernen* boat club and the *Amager Strand* allotment association, lies a little bathhouse. Called 'Little Helgoland' (*Lille Helgoland*) it certainly lives up to its name: it's still painted in the same special Flügger turquoise as the original, and much larger, 'Helgoland Bath' which is located just a few hundred metres further south.

Dropping by this miniature version of the Helgoland Bath and stepping out on to the jetty for a while is a memorable experience, which you can enjoy both in summer and in winter. In winter, the bathhouse heroically braves the elements, standing shivering in the icy cold with the beautiful colours of the wintry sea as a backdrop. In summer, a walk along the jetty invites you to enjoy the bathhouse and the lovely sea views beyond.

Little Helgoland was only intended to be a temporary replacement for the somewhat dilapidated, hundred year-old Helgoland Bath, which was demolished during the construction of Amager Beach and finally rebuilt in 2008.

Little Helgoland finally also survived and it still stands: a plucky little survivor, which still welcomes its visitors.

OPEN-AIR SCHOOL ❻

Skolen ved Sundet
Samosvej 50, 2300 S
• Access from Samosvej and Sumatravej
• Metro: Amager Strand

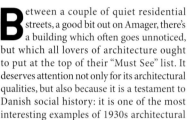

The "Weak Children's School", a small masterpiece of Danish modernism

Between a couple of quiet residential streets, a good bit out on Amager, there's a building which often goes unnoticed, but which all lovers of architecture ought to put at the top of their "Must See" list. It deserves attention not only for its architectural qualities, but also because it is a testament to Danish social history: it is one of the most interesting examples of 1930s architectural design being tailored to the needs of the most vulnerable in society.

The Open-Air School was completed in 1938 in conjunction with the next-door School by the Sound (*Skolen ved Sundet*). The architect was Kaj Gottlob, best known by the locals for his design of the Knippelsbro Bridge in 1937 and the Langebro Bridge in 1954.

The Open-Air School, also known as the "Weak Children's School" (*Svagbørnsskolen*), was built to accommodate a total of 144 students. They were then divided into classes of twenty-four and each class was allocated one of the school's six classrooms. The classrooms were situated on the ground floor of the school with direct access to the south-facing garden. As the school's nickname suggests, it was built to take care of the city's physically weak and malnourished children.

As the school provided daily meals for the children, a dining room, a kitchen and a special apartment for the cook were all built close to the classrooms. Every day after lunch, the children had to take a nap for an hour and a half in the first-floor dormitories. In order to let in as much light and warmth as possible, all the windows faced south. The glass panels were designed so that they could slide sideways to let in fresh air. In addition, the dormitory's roof could be partially opened. The school also had a medical centre which gave the children "light-baths", thus ensuring that they were exposed to the health-giving rays of the sun.

The building served as the "Weak Children's School" until the problem lessened in the 1950s. Later it accommodated children with behavioural difficulties until, more recently, it was turned into a school for physically disabled children, who are integrated into the classes at a nearby school as much as possible.

KASTRUP VÆRK

❼

Today called Bryggergården
Bryggergården 1–21, 2770 Kastrup
• Metro: Femøren

Copenhagen's oldest existing industrial complex

Not far from Amager Strandvej, half-hidden behind tall trees, Kastrup Værk is today the oldest surviving industrial complex in Copenhagen. Although the place is surrounded by busy traffic, it is still uncharted territory for many locals. The complex, set behind two large gates, consists of two rows of beautiful buildings, which share a common cobbled courtyard.

The developer of its oldest part, Jacob Fortling, was one of the most entrepreneurial men in 18th-century Copenhagen. At the age of 18, he left Germany for the Danish capital, where he quickly progressed from working as a stonemason to becoming court architect, and, in 1747, he received a royal charter to quarry limestone on Saltholm; this quarry was the foundation of Kastrup Værk.

He set up what was to become his business empire on a headland off Amager's east coast and here he established a port, a limestone factory and brick factories, and a plant for the manufacture of faïence and stoneware. From this base he supplied the city's sugar refineries with moulds, building projects with materials, and the nobility and bourgeoisie with his fine faïence ware. He showed off the latter to clients in a high-ceilinged display room, which still exists today in the building (now known as *Slottet*, meaning *the palace*).

He also built his private residence, called Kastrup Gård, in the nearby village of Kastrup and connected it to Kastrup Værk via a beautifully landscaped avenue. Whereas Kastrup Gård still exists, the avenue has long since disappeared.

Fortling died in 1761, at just 50 years of age, but the manufacturing of faïence continued until 1800, and the limestone works lasted until 1955. From 1838 to 1905, the buildings also housed a brewery which gave it its present name of Bryggergården.

THE MYSTERIOUS EAGLE AND THE SWASTIKA

Recently, a shop has moved into one of the buildings. On its rear wall there is a finely painted German eagle and a swastika which the shop owner has discreetly hidden behind a piece of furniture. The eagle and the swastika were most likely painted during World War II, when the nearby Kastrup harbour was occupied by German soldiers.

SALTHOLM ISLAND

5 km off the coast of Amager
Due to the island's environment, traffic is prohibited on its southern tip
(at *Svaneklapperne*); in the main part of the island (from *Holmegaard*
southwards) traffic is prohibited from 1 April to 15 July.
• Visits can be arranged through *Saltholm Ejerlaug*
• www.saltholm.dk

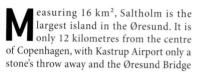

A corner of paradise

Measuring 16 km², Saltholm is the largest island in the Øresund. It is only 12 kilometres from the centre of Copenhagen, with Kastrup Airport only a stone's throw away and the Øresund Bridge almost within reach. The nuclear power plant at Barsebäck is also nearby, right on the Swedish coast, and gigantic cruise and container ships glide steadily past in a constant stream. Despite being surrounded by all this activity, however, Saltholm is a true natural paradise, even if every time you raise your eyes you catch a glimpse of the city.

When you arrive in Saltholm and go ashore at *Barakkebroen*, you should definitely pay a visit to the bird observation tower by *Barakkegården*. From here you can get a fine view over the entire island, for it is as flat as it can possibly be – and virtually without trees. Most of the island is between one and two metres above sea level, making it an easy target for flooding, and at certain times during the winter months as much as two-thirds of it can be under water. For the same reason, in 1820, a series of small hills was built as refuges for the island's population of hares.

Perhaps precisely because of its location, where it is assailed by noise on all sides, but yet remains a haven of peace, a visit to Saltholm is a unique experience. Consequently, if you meet someone on your trip, there is a good chance that it is a visitor just over for the day, typically one with an interest in botany or ornithology, or both. Saltholm is home to some rare species of plants. It is one of the very few places in Northern Europe where the Blue Iris grows wild and it is also host to a humbler, more inconspicuous, but a still very rare, species of the mouse-ear chickweed.

However, Saltholm is probably best known for its birdlife; the island is considered to have Denmark's densest population of birds, including northern Europe's largest colony of eider ducks. The number of birds, both breeding, roosting and migratory, is counted annually in the hundreds of thousands. In addition, hares are to be found all over the island, and, if you are at the coast, keep a lookout for seals.

Since the Middle Ages, when Saltholm was first inhabited, the island has been used for grazing animals, and, during the summer months, there are up to 1,000 cows and a few sheep to be seen peacefully cropping its grass.

SALTHOLM MUSEUM

The museum is situated right across from Barakkegården in the
Stenladen building
• Admission: free

*"Perhaps
from a dinosaur?"*

When you are on Saltholm, a visit to
the island's museum is a must. It was
opened in 1998 by a local man, Hans
Zimling, who lived on the island all his life. Its
collection is more a cabinet of curiosities than
a standard display of artefacts.

The museum's purpose is to introduce visitors to the history of Saltholm
and to act as a record of its interesting past. Many of the items have been
washed ashore; however, the information about them is rather limited and you
miss hearing the voice of a local like Hans Zimling putting the pieces of the
puzzle together and telling you the stories behind the exhibits. You are not left
completely in the dark though, as some information is available and it's quite
fun to try and make sense of the rather chaotic collection.

The information itself is very eclectic, and very personal to the island.
Some of it is displayed on a blackboard which outlines important episodes
from Saltholm's past, namely: the first time the name *Saltholm* appeared
in the historical record in 1230; its use as a quarantine centre during the
plague years from 1709 to 1715; and the abandonment of plans to construct
a new Copenhagen airport there. Some exhibits have little information on
the labels while others are accompanied by handwritten signs done in thick
black marker pen. These ones are very quirky and very local, for example:
"perhaps from a dinosaur"; "this paper knife is made of wood from the Battle
of Copenhagen in 1801"; "20 mineral water bottles, all found on the beach at
Saltholm"; or "from a horse who died on Saltholm".

There is also a wonderful selection of bits and pieces of island life: fishing
equipment and agricultural tools, charts, drainage pumps from the island's
limestone quarries, clogs and boots, animal bones and skulls, and, of course,
the flotsam and jetsam washed ashore on its beaches – lifebuoys and
driftwood.

As it is located midway between Denmark and Sweden in the middle of the
main navigation route between the Baltic countries and the rest of the world,
Saltholm has always been a focal point for the large and small events in Danish
history, and this charming little local museum is a touching and personal
display of this.

ALPHABETICAL INDEX

ALPHABETICAL INDEX

Acknowledgements:

Our thanks to:

Mogens Andersen, June Baatsch, Poul H. Beck, Hans Bendixen, Linda Bruun, Erling Christensen, Lars Christensen, Jakob Dahl, Michael Dinesen, Søren Ekman, Merete Femø, Jan Frederiksen, Adam Grandjean, Birger Søby Hansen, Connie Hansen, Ida Haugsted, Klaus Henningsen, Jesper Lundgaard Johansen, Palle Banks Jørgensen, Laura Kabongo, Claus Kofod, Isabel Vela Laier, Egon Langbøl, Marianne Lohse, Jens Monefeldt Ludvigsen, Michael Lundquist, Steffen Løvkjær, Lene Midtgaard, Ulla Mollerup, Svend-Aage Lyhne Nielsen, Jens Nieman, Erik Nillausen, Marianne Pedersen, Kenneth Illum Petersen, Sergij Plekhov, Merete Pelle Poulsen, Banja Rathnov, Ed Romein, Kristoffer Sahlholdt, Jørgen Saustrup, Anne Jonstrup Simonsen, Helle Skyggebjerg, Hans Henrik Smedegaard, Jesper Sonne, Joyce Svensson, Finn Syndbjerg, Dennis Sørensen, Michael Sørensen, Hans Tybjerg, Margrethe Wiwel.

Text credits:

Ex-Orient Bar is written by Linda Lapina.

Photo credits:

All photos by Andrea Kabongo, Johanne Steenstrup and Klaus Dahl, except:
Cover page (Balloon hangar): Iben Bølling Kaufmann. Frederiksborg stuffed horse: Thorkild Jensen. The Aurora painting: Kenneth Illum Petersen. Queen's Box at the Reformed Church: Roberto Fortuna. Portrait of J. F. Struensee (The marble bathtub): DKKS, Rosenborg Slot. The centre of Frederiksberg Garden: Styrelsen for Slotte og Kulturejendomme. Altarbread bakery at the Deaconess Diakonissestiftelsen: Sille Arendt/kirkenikbh.dk. N. H. Rasmussen's gymnasium: Jens Hemmel. Tuberculosis sheds (historic photo): Holger Damgaard/POLFOTO. Bat walks in Fælledparken: Amalie Rosa Maegaard. The mysterious eagle and the swastika (Kastrup Værk): Chris Tonnessen.

Maps: **Cyrille Suss** - Layout design: **Roland Deloi** - Layout: **Stéphanie Benoit** - Translation: **Caroline Lawrence** - Editing: **Marjorie Horn** and **Jana Gough** - Proofreading: **Kimberly Bess**